Festival and Joy

Biblical Encounters Series

Suffering by Erhard S. Gerstenberger and Wolfgang Schrage
Translated by John E. Steely

Festival and Joy

**Eckart Otto
and
Tim Schramm**

Biblical Encounters Series

Translated by James L. Blevins

87-1690

ABINGDON
Nashville

Fest und Freude

© 1977 Verlag W. Kohlhammer

Festival and Joy

Translation copyright © 1980 by Abingdon

Library of Congress Cataloging in Publication Data

OTTO, ECKART.
  Festival and joy.
  (Biblical encounters series)
  Translation of Fest und Freude.
  Bibliography: p.
1. Fasts and feasts—Biblical teaching.   2 Joy—
Biblical teaching. I.   Schramm, Tim, 1940- joint
author.   II.   Title.   III.   Series.
BS680.F370'8713   264   80-12532

ISBN 0-687-12940-0

MANUFACTURED BY THE PARTHENON PRESS AT
NASHVILLE, TENNESSEE, UNITED STATES OF AMERICA

Contents

CONTENTS

INTRODUCTION

Fear is a feeling which determines our time; fear narrows the vision, reduces thoughts and emotions, and blocks the way to communication with others. It robs the future and also hinders the perception of the possibilities of the present. Fear doubts the meaning of the individual life as well as all life in general.

Fear will be replaced by joy. Joy cannot be commanded, rather it must be established. The basis of joy is meaning. Meaning is experienced and communicated in festivity. Texts from the Old and New Testament used in this book speak of the experience of overcoming fear. The joy which overcomes fear occurs in the Old Testament almost always in the cultic fest, while in the New Testament it takes place in "the everyday world." The biblical witness tells us that festivity and joy contend always anew and once and for all against fear, sorrow, and death. Faith sees within that festivity God's intent for salvation and rejoices at its closeness. To encounter such faith and to hear its demands seem to us to be a very promising venture.

A.
FESTIVAL AND JOY IN THE OLD TESTAMENT

I. Passover

The proto-Israelite seminomadic tribes, such as the tribes of Abraham, Isaac, and Jacob, moved every year to the cultivated land for a change of pasture from the steppes, which had been made arid by the sun and the hot east wind blowing out of the inner desert. They came there in order to graze their cattle in the harvested fields. In the fall with the beginning of the rainy season, as the steppes sprouted a sparse vegetation, these nomads and their cattle left the cultivated land to return again to the steppes, only once again the next spring to repeat the cycle. The way into the cultivated land could be the beginning of a dangerous journey for there disputes awaited with other seminomadic tribes, perhaps concerning the use of a well (Gen. 26:15 ff) or ambushes by the inhabitants of the land (Gen. 20:2 ff; 26:7 ff). Would one always be able to find grazing pastures along the way? Would one encounter surprise attacks on life and property? The setting out in the spring was a setting out into uncertainty. The question arises how this situation was expressed in the cult of the seminomads.

1. The Passover Tradition, Exodus 12:21-24

Israel's origin in the cultivated land of Palestine, as recent Old Testament historical critical work has increasingly demonstrated, was a complicated process extending over many centuries. It was much more involved than the picture portrayed in the books of the Hexateuch, Genesis—Joshua. Hence the Israelite cult also had a complex early history that can hardly be traced historically to Moses alone, as the founder of the religion. Rather, it had its origins in pre-Israelite time in the nomadic life-style and among the inhabitants of the Canaanite cultivated land. Corresponding to this, it is also not possible to determine the specifics of the Israelitic cult, or as a consequence that of the Christian cult, without first bringing in the background of the cultural history of the Middle Eastern religions on which the development of the Yahweh religion of Israel was dependent and rooted. With the Passover we turn to the clearest example of the nomadic cult, which has as its basic function the dealing with reality. However, we find no connection to a holy site. As a primitive cult, it was not a festival in the strictest sense of the word. Yet, the Passover in its nomadic origins belongs in this cultic connection, and this very origin in the history of religions clarifies Israel's attempt to deal with cultic reality in Yahweh.

The oldest tradition available to us which demonstrates signs of the nomadic Passover is found in Exodus 12:21-24:

> (21) Then Moses called for all the elders of Israel, and said unto them, "Draw out and take you a lamb according to your families, and kill the passover. (22) And you shall take a bunch of hyssop, and dip it in the blood that is in the basin, and strike the lintel and the two side posts with the blood that is in the basin; and none of you shall go out at the door of his house until the morning. (23) For Yahweh will pass through to smite the Egyptians; and when he sees the blood upon the lintel, and on the two side posts, Yahweh will pass over the door, and will not suffer the destroyer to come in unto your houses to smite you. (24) And you shall observe this thing for an ordinance to you and to your sons for ever."

From the form-critical point of view, Exodus 12:21-24 is viewed as a unity and on the basis of syntax is placed in the classification of "ritual" (the formation of the verbs in the perfect tense in connection with "and," Hebrew *waw* [61.77 ff]*). As I have demonstrated in another place [83.3 ff], this Passover ritual

---

*The numbers shown in the text indicate the numbers that are found in the Bibliography.

tradition has been added in the context of the plague cycle that originally belonged to the Matzoth Festival, for the Passover ritual could hardly have been derived from the situation of the Exodus out of Egypt. We are, therefore, directed to answer the questions concerning the origin of the Passover ritual tradition by looking within it and its expressed cultic horizon.

2. The Passover Ritual

According to the history of traditions, the Passover ritual tradition of Exodus 12:21-24 is an independent unity and is separate from the plague cycle. It shows traces of a history of traditions' process of interpretation. In reference to verse 22b, the phrase "and none of you shall go out at the door of his house until the morning" is missing and stands in contrast to the introduction (verse 21) where all Israel is addressed rather than the elders. In verse 23: "For Yahweh will pass through to smite the Egyptians; and when he sees the blood upon the lintel, and on the two side posts, Yahweh will pass over the door, and will not suffer the destroyer to come in unto your houses to smite you." It is obvious that in the first section of the verse Yahweh himself passes through to slay the Egyptians, whereas in the second section the "destroyer" has this function of slaying Egyptians. Yahweh hinders him from slaying the Israelites. The destroyer is a demon, a fact that points to an origin of the Passover ritual that is independent of any connection with Yahweh. The original connection was worded in such a way that the demon of the destroyer was prevented from entering, attacking, or causing calamity. From a history of traditions' point of view, Yahweh is introduced secondarily and the destroyer helps him carry out his plans. We are thus pointed to a pre-Israelitic and pre-Yahweh origin of the Passover ritual.

Thereby, the question should be asked whether a pre-Israelitic, nomadic sphere of life is indicated.

The thesis, represented especially by I. Engnell [26.39 ff] and J. B. Segal [98.117 ff], that the Passover was derived from the New Year's festival of the cultivated land, is based on the theory that the Passover and Matzoth Festivals constitute a cultic historical unity. This cannot be sustained exegetically. The Passover was, in its most ancient form as seen in Exodus 12:21-24, a ritual that was not attached to a holy place, but rather, as verse 21 ff shows, it was celebrated in the tribal relation of the larger family. This setting of the oldest Passover tradition points rather to a nomadic origin.

This connection is confirmed by the Passover tradition of the priestly document (fifth-fourth centuries B.C.). In Exodus 12:1-14 the garment donned during the Passover was like typical shepherd's clothing, girded about, with sandals and crook, attributes of the nomadic herdsmen. The bitter herbs were typical desert plants [105.15]. However, one must be careful in viewing the Passover tradition in the P document as the source for the pre-Israelitic Passover practice, for P's interest in the postexilic period must be taken into account [70.131 ff]. But it is significant that P rightly connects the Passover with characteristically nomadic themes.

In the midpoint of the nomadic Passover stood an apotropaic blood ritual. The Passover ritual placed no weight upon determining how the small cattle were to be slaughtered or what was to happen with the meat. At this pre-Israelitic step of the Passover ritual tradition, we still find no word of a Passover sacrifice. The purpose of the slaughter was to attain the necessary blood for the Passover ritual. This blood was caught in a bowl. With a whisk of hyssop plant the blood was spread around the entrance of the nomadic dwelling, the tent. The hyssop, which was supposed to prevent any contact with blood and its apotropaic power. Blood belonged in its setting to a superhuman secretive sphere. The blood was applied to the

entrance of the tent, because the destroyer was expected on
Passover night and the calamity that he brought to man and
animal could be kept away. Thereby, the question is raised
concerning the function that the Passover had in controlling life
and conquering reality among the nomadic pre-Israelites.

3. The Experience of Reality in the Passover

A. Alt [2.139 ff and elsewhere] has made clear the
significance of the changing of pastures in the life of the
pre-Israelitic nomadic herdsmen in the area of Syria-Palestine.
These tribal bands moved deeply into the cultivated land at the
beginning of the summer dry season when the vegetation on
the steppes began to die. There they found in the harvested
fields pasture ground for their goats and fatty-tailed sheep.
During the winter rainy season they dwelled on the steppelike
zones between the desert and the cultivated land. The rhythm
of this annual change of pasture determined the life of these
herdsmen. The setting out for the cultivated land in the spring
and the return journey to the steppes in the fall constituted very
important events set apart from everyday life. The Passover
ritual [93.205 ff] belongs in the context of the preparation for
setting out from the steppes to the cultivated land in the spring.
Its setting is in the night when they set out from the steppes. In
that night uncertainty prevailed. How would the journey go?
Would man and beast survive or be overcome by the numerous
threatening dangers? The future in this moment of setting out
appeared uncertain and endangered. Would one always find
wells and pastures at the right time? Would one confront hostile
enemies—competing nomads—and be able to live peaceably
with one another? This situation required a special ritualistic
assurance in order to safeguard man and beast. In this night of
uncertainty and danger the destroyer went about and
threatened both man and beast. The destroyer, personalized as

a demon, symbolized the uncertainty and danger involved in setting out to the new pastures. In a very concrete way he was anchored to the developing Passover traditions. P. Laaf [70.155] has proposed that the Passover ritual was used to ward off the demons of the desert who would not allow the nomadic tribes to leave their dominion in the steppes without some hindrance. The key, however, lies in the question why the seminomads left the steppes exactly at the time of the spring's full moon and journeyed into the cultivated land. In answer to this question O. Keel [56.414 ff] has contributed an interesting point. He has demonstrated that the expectation of a demonic destroyer was inferred from the observation that every year in the spring, the hot east wind suddenly appeared (Arab—*eš šerqīje*), caused the vegetation to die, and brought with it danger to man and beast. The appearance of this hot [like a hair dryer] east wind forced them to journey to the cultivated land. This wind was attributed to demonic-destructive powers from which one could be protected by an apotropaic ritual.

A comparison to the *radšab*-sacrifice, which took place during the spring months, affords even fewer possibilities [40.389 ff]. It had a pre-Islamic nomadic origin. The *radšab* festival was celebrated in the life sphere of the shepherds; it was a family festival in which the oldest family member presided and sacrificed a small animal. If there are parallel aspects in the relationship of the cultural milieu of *radšab* with the Passover, there still exists the difficulty of attempting to trace back a common cultural-historical root for both of them. For in *radšab* the sacrifice stood in the midpoint, but in the Passover, an apotropaic blood ritual. In *radšab* one often debated whether the sacrifice was of the firstborn or of a one-year-old, but it was not concerned just with firstborn animals [105.9]. Rather the *dahiba* slaughtering points back to a pre-Islamic time and a common root with the Passover [47.337 ff]. When the shepherd moved into a new tent, the demon, who claimed that flock for himself, must be prevented from destructive activity.

For this reason an apotropaic blood ritual was required. At the entrance to the tent a small animal's jugular vein was cut and the blood that streamed out was caught. The center part of the tent was painted with this blood. This ritual was also used by those who had already settled on the land. Upon moving into a new house, they would paint the lintel of the door with blood and sprinkle it also on the door.

If the function of Passover is placed in the social context of nomadic life, then it is valid to view it within the context of the history of religions. A very old step of the Passover tradition, which can still be reconstructed from Exodus 12:21-24, points to a pre-Israelitic nomadic level of the tradition in which Yahweh had not yet been linked to the ritual. A. Alt [1.1 ff] should be credited for our knowledge of the religious norms of the nomadic ancestors of Israel. These nomadic tribes honored a divinity who had revealed himself in a promise to one of their ancestors and to his descendants. Since this divinity had revealed himself in an ancestor, he was thought to be present in the bloodline of the family and was thus characterized as God of my/your fathers. In Abraham one came to know the tribal father who had received a promise that, in turn, affected the whole tribe. This was also true of Isaac and Jacob in their tribes. The Canaanite gods of the cultivated land were different from this nomadic god who had no established place of culture, but accompanied and led the nomadic tribes on their journeys. In this way he assured the promise to the descendants and the responsibility of the survival of the tribe.

However, we ought not to centralize the religious concepts of reality in such a monotheistic way of those who reverenced the gods of their fathers, as Alt would have us do. It has already been shown that the earliest step of the Passover tradition in Exodus 12:21-24 was transmitted by a nomadic ancestor of Israel and that the apotropaic Passover ritual had its setting in the sphere of changing pasture. If this thesis, widely recognized in Old Testament research, is correct then we can conclude that the nomadic patriarchal tribes developed through a long process, which involved the wanderers becoming settlers of the land and finally the Israel who worshiped Yahweh. In this way the Passover of the nomads, who wandered from pasture to pasture, came to Israel and was transmitted further. Thus, we contend that these nomadic tribes who revered the gods of their divine fathers were forerunners of Israel and also celebrated an apotropaic Passover ritual. These tribes recognized, in addition to the gods of the fathers, a whole world of other numinous appearances, even the demon of the destroyer.

It is obvious that the nomads did not overcome the dangers of their exposed position in breaking camp by reciting the promises of their patriarchal god for the continued life of the tribe. That would be an almost too modern view of the possibilities of dealing with life among oriental tribes. The appearance of the sudden east wind that burned the vegetation was the signal for breaking camp and setting out. This east wind was traced back quite often to a demon whom the patriarchal god could not battle. By the magical effect of blood's life power, the destructive activity of the demon was warded off for both man and beast.

The limitations of this form of experiencing and dealing with reality in the pre-Yahwistic nomadic period are obvious. The apotropaic cult celebration opened up no future dimension. It was concerned only with introducing the magical power of the blood to ward off the annual threat of demonic danger, the regular appearance of the destroyer. This form of nomadic ritual could not transcend a cyclical type of reality which was determined on the one hand by demonic attack and on the other by an apotropaic magical practice that protected one from the threat. In the pre-Israelitic nomadic cult one could not conceive of an historical dimension in which permanent protection could be found against threats to man and beast. They possessed no concept of promise-fulfillment. The cult did not yet have the function of relating God's acts and experience to historical experience. It was difficult for them to understand God as one who changes reality.

4. The Passover in Relation to Yahweh Worship

The annual change of pastures accomplished by the nomadic tribes of the Syrian-Palestinian area lead, in the second half of the second millennium, to a gradual settling of the cultivated land. One tribe would settle here, another there, in areas thinly populated by the inhabitants of the land, such as in the Palestinian mountain region. During the summer they established themselves and never returned again to the steppes. In the course of this complicated and lengthy process of "taking the land," which stretched over many centuries, the Passover ritual also came to the cultivated land. Nevertheless, the social and cultural situation of the original nomadic tradition changed in the process; the nomads became the settled inhabitants of the land and carried on agriculture. There was then no longer the annual setting out from the steppes for the cultivated land. There was also no demonic destroyer appearing in the east wind of the steppe, bringing death to the vegetation and the need for protection. In the new situation of the settled life in the cultivated land, the Passover ritual lost its relation to the basic life experience of the nomads.

The tribes from the steppes, which settled in on the land in the course of their development, came into contact with two very significant manifestations of the history of religions. At the end of that course stands the union of tribes called Israel. The one manifestation centered around Bethlehem and the nomadic tribe of Judah, which brought the worship of Yahweh from the desert at Sinai into the cultivated land and spread it about. The other manifestation stemmed from a group of ethnically related refugees from Egypt who settled in Palestine and viewed themselves as delivered from their Egyptian oppressors by a miraculous event. The Yahweh of Sinai was understood then in the Sea of Reeds' miracle as the God of deliverance. Thus, he was experienced as a God who reached into historical reality and changed it. The confession of the Exodus from Egypt became the primitive confession of the tribes of Israel [79.50 ff], which came into being in the cultivated land. In the cultic reenactment of this basic fact of salvation history, the Passover ritual found a new setting. On the basis of a thematic relationship, both the ritual of the Passover and the Exodus from Egypt concerned themselves with a setting-out situation—a wandering to the cultivated land of Palestine. Only now it was not the annual setting out from the steppes into the cultivated land, but rather the setting out from Egypt to wander through the desert, which eventually would lead to Palestine. Setting out no longer was a matter of protection from the annual threat of the destroyer, but rather the realization of a unique act of God in salvation history. Yahweh must now be introduced anew into the Passover ritual as the one actually acting. The destroyer was reinterpreted as one who helped Yahweh fulfill his promises by carrying out destructive acts against the foe. The motif of the nomadic Passover that the destroyer was warded off by an apotropaic blood ritual was subordinated to a history of salvation theme. Now Yahweh struck his enemies, the Egyptians, through the destroyer. The blood on the doors of the houses of Yahweh's people, the Israelites, no longer served as a magical protection, but rather as a distinctive mark in the history of salvation.

In the history of religions, it is frequently observed that a ritual is carried out in a new historical and social context as a rite but receives a new interpretation. The reinterpretation of the Passover ritual in the realm of salvation history in reference to Yahweh shows a changed understanding of reality and a new level of cultic perceiving and dealing with reality. The magical effect was no longer sought in the blood ritual, but rather was realized cultically in the unique event of salvation history, grounded in the past and made present in Yahweh's reaching into history to bring salvation. Thus, in the blood ritual of the Passover, the salvation effect of the Exodus was realized in the everyday life of Israel in the cultivated land. If, therefore, the tribes of Israel, occupying the land, slaughtered the Passover lamb every year in the spring and completed the blood ritual, then the deliverance from the Exodus became a cultic reality in the cultivated land. In the course of a year this was realized and preserved as deliverance to salvation. The protection that Israel experienced through Yahweh in the Exodus was reenacted every year in the cultivated land through the Passover.

Here for the first time we recognize an essential framework for Israel's dealing with reality in the cult. A salvation event of Yahweh's dealing with Israel is brought into the present and possesses the power to renew reality. In addition it spreads a blessing throughout the course of the coming year. A past salvation event becomes realized in the present and radiates its salvation effectiveness into the future.

In the Exodus, Israel experienced Yahweh as a powerful God who changed historical reality, and this knowledge was brought to bear on the cult. Israel no longer adhered to the magical view of the pre-Israelite nomadic Passover, which was expressed in a cyclical understanding of reality. The subject was no longer a dialectical one of demonic threat and magical practice, but rather the making present of the salvific act of Yahweh with Israel. This in turn became the pledge of salvation for the future.

The mood in the old apotropaic ritual of the nomads was enveloped in fear. One had to ward off the harmful effects of the destroyer from one's tent. But would the magical power of the blood be sufficient to ward off destruction? This fearful question must have always stood in the background. In contrast, how great was the stride that Israel made in understanding reality and dealing with life by experiencing a God, Yahweh, who had acted in history. There was no longer a need for a magical warding off of disaster. Much more one could experience in history an actual divine changing of reality. The Israelite could be caught up in a salvific happening from the past. This divine happening could be realized in the present through the cult, but yet was also at work in the future and in every encounter determined everyday life. Therefore, joy and hope characterized the mood of the Passover celebration in Israel.

In Exodus 12:25-27a the Passover tradition in the course of its transmission in Israel experienced a paraenetic expansion.

> (25) And when you come to the land which Yahweh will give you, as he promised, you shall keep this service. (26) And when your children say to you, "What do you mean by this service?" (27a) You shall say, "It is the sacrifice of Yahweh's Passover (*zaebăh*), for he passed over the houses of the people of Israel in Egypt, when he slew the Egyptians, but spared our house."

It is difficult to determine when this addition was added to the Passover ritual, but one can say with a certain degree of assurance that this happened before the reform of Josiah in the seventh century B.C. This is evident from the language used [83.18, note 56]. This date is also affirmed by the fact that no mention is made of the connection between the Passover and the Matzoth celebration and the centralization of this celebration in the sanctuary of Jerusalem.

This paraenetic addition demonstrates a development of the Passover within the context of the history of cults. In the Israel of the cultivated land the blood ritual was no longer understood magically or apotropaically but was reinterpreted as a distinctive sign within the history of salvation. For that reason a community sacrifice (*zaebăh*) took on central focus in which the fatty parts of the sacrificial animal were sacrificed to

Yahweh while the flesh was consumed in a common meal. There Yahweh was thought to be present in invisible form. In this joyful, unrestrained sacrificial meal, the community was established, a community of celebrating ones with Yahweh and one another. The salvation power of the Exodus miracle was experienced, therefore, increasingly in a community sacrifice, in which Yahweh of the Reeds Sea miracle was understood as present in the meal in his salvation activity and power.

II. The Matzoth Festival

The proto-Israelite tribes from the desert became established in the cultivated land. Another group leaving Egypt, composed of Israelite tribes honoring Yahweh of Sinai, encountered them. And now the problems confronting the Israelites were increased; the shepherds had become farmers, but the land that they farmed was not their own. Did not the inhabitants who had lived there for centuries have the exclusive right to the land? And the question must be asked, Were not the inhabitants' gods the lords of the land, not Yahweh the God of Sinai? These questions must have been pressing ones as the Israelites encountered or mixed with the inhabitants of the land, and eventually these led to a struggle for the possession of the land. Above all, the Israelites settled only the thinly inhabited mountain ranges. Here the land soon became scarce. But the tribes of Israel could not move into the fruitful plains for there the more militarily powerful Canaanite city states ruled the territory. How could this political situation be harmonized with the knowledge that Yahweh was Lord of the land? We will see how these problems were addressed to the Holy One of Israel in festive events of the premonarchical period.

1. Traditions of the Matzoth Festival in Joshua 3–5

(5:10) While the people of Israel were encamped in Gilgal (they kept the Passover on the fourteenth day of the month at evening) in the plains of Jericho. (11) (And on the morrow after the Passover) (on that very day), they ate of the produce of the land, unleavened cakes and parched grain. (12) And the manna ceased on the morrow, when they ate of the produce of the land; and the people of Israel had manna no more, but ate of the fruit of the land of Canaan that year.

The Gilgal Matzoth tradition, Joshua 5:10-12, as shown by its language, belongs in the pre-Deuteronomic time. From the point of view of the history of traditions, it is secondary and has been expanded by the Passover theme [81.175 ff]. These expansions were set off in parentheses in the material just quoted. This tradition of a Matzoth Festival in Gilgal rests on certain grounds in the history of traditions [81.26 ff].[1] We have a further Matzoth tradition in Joshua 3–4 in the redaction of two sources. One source, A, should be dated in the time of the kings and represents in part the historical work of the Yahwist. Source B should be dated in the period of the exile.

Pre-Deuteronomic Source A (J)

(3:1) Early in the morning Joshua rose and set out from Shittim, with all the people of Israel; and they came to the Jordan, and lodged there before they passed over. (3:5) And Joshua said to the people, "Sanctify yourselves, for tomorrow Yahweh will do wonders among you." (3:9) "Come hither, and hear the words of Yahweh your God." (3:10) And Joshua said, "Hereby you shall know that the living God is among you, and that he will without fail drive out from before you the Canaanites, the Hittites, the Hivites, the Perizzites, the Girgashites, the Amorites, and the Jebusites. (3:11) Behold, the ark of the covenant of Yahweh of all the earth is to pass over before you into the Jordan. (3:12) Now therefore take twelve men from the tribes of Israel from each tribe a man."

(4:4) Then Joshua called the twelve men from the people of Israel, whom he had appointed, a man from each tribe; (4:5) and Joshua said to them, "Pass on before the ark of Yahweh your God into the midst of the Jordan, and take up each of you a stone upon his shoulder, according to the number of the tribes of the people of Israel, (4:6) that this may be a sign among you, when your children ask in time to come, 'What do these stones mean to you?' (4:7) Then you shall tell them that the waters of the Jordan were cut off before the ark of the covenant of Yahweh; when it passed over the Jordan, the waters of the Jordan were cut off. So these stones shall be to the people of Israel a memorial forever!" (4:9) And Joshua set up twelve stones in the midst of the Jordan, in the place where the feet of the priests bearing the ark of the covenant had stood; and they are there to this day. (4:10 *a, b*) For the priests who bore the ark stood in the midst of the Jordan, until everything was finished that Yahweh commanded Joshua to tell the people. The people passed over in haste, (4:11*b*) and the priests passed over before the people.

Deuteronomic Source B

(1:10) Then Joshua commanded the officers of the people, (11) "Pass through the camp, and command the people, 'Prepare your provisions; for within three days you are to pass over this Jordan, to go in to take possession of the land which Yahweh your God gives you to possess.' " (3:2) At the end of three days the officers went through the camp (3) and commanded the people, "When you see the ark of the covenant of Yahweh your God being carried by the Levitical priests, then you shall set out from your place and follow it (4*d,e*) that you may know the way you shall go, for you have not passed this way before." And Joshua said to the priests, "Take up the ark of the covenant, and pass on before the people." And they took up the ark of the covenant and went before the people. (7) And Yahweh said to Joshua, "This day I will begin to exalt you in the sight of all Israel, that they may know that, as I was with Moses, so I will be with you. (8) And you shall command the priests who bear the ark of the covenant, 'When you come to the brink of the waters of the Jordan, you shall stand still in the Jordan.' " (3:13) "And when the soles of the feet of the priests who bear the ark of Yahweh the Lord of all the earth, shall rest in the waters of the Jordan, the waters of the Jordan shall be stopped from flowing, and the waters coming down from above shall stand in one heap." (14) So, when the people set out from their tents, to pass over the Jordan with the priests bearing the ark of the covenant before the people, (15) and when those who bore the ark had come to the Jordan, and the feet of the priests bearing the ark were dipped in the brink of the water (the Jordan overflows all its banks throughout the time of harvest), (16) the waters coming down from above stood and rose up in a heap far off, at Adam, the city that is beside Zarenthan, and those flowing down toward the Sea of Arabah, the Salt Sea, were wholly cut off; and the people passed over opposite Jericho, (3.17 ab) and while all Israel were passing over on dry ground, the priests who bore the ark of the covenant of the Lord stood on dry ground in the midst of the Jordan. (4:1b) Yahweh said to Joshua, (4:2) "Take twelve men from the people, from each tribe a man (4:3) and command them, 'Take twelve stones from here out of the Jordan, from the very place where the priests' feet stood, and carry them over with you, and lay them down in the place where you lodge tonight.'" (4:8) And the men of Israel did as Joshua commanded, and took up twelve stones out of the midst of the Jordan, according to the number of the tribes of the people of Israel, as Yahweh told Joshua; and they carried them over with them to the place where they lodged and laid them down there. (4:11) And . . . when all the people had finished passing over, the ark of Yahweh and the priests passed over. (4:12) The sons of Reuben and the sons of Gad and the half tribe of Manasseh passed over armed before the people of Israel as Moses had bidden them. (4:13) About forty thousand ready armed for war passed over before the Lord for battle, to the plains of Jericho. (4:14) On that day the Lord exalted Joshua in the sight of all Israel; and they stood in awe of him, as they had stood in awe of Moses, all the days of his life. (4:18b) The waters of the Jordan returned to their place and overflowed all its banks, as before. (4:19) The people came up out of the Jordan . . . and they encamped in Gilgal on the east border of Jericho. (4:20) And those twelve stones which they took out of the Jordan, Joshua set up in Gilgal. (4:21) And he said to the people of Israel, "When your children ask their fathers in time to come, 'What do

these stones mean?' (4:22) Then you should let your children
know, 'Israel passed over this Jordan on dry ground.' (4:23) For
Yahweh your God dried up the waters of the Jordan for you
until you passed over, as Yahweh your God did to the Red Sea,
which he dried up for us until we passed over, (4:24) so that all
the peoples of the earth may know that the hand of Yahweh is
mighty; that you may fear Yahweh your God for ever."

As I have shown in another place, chapters 1–11 in Joshua have
been edited from a pre-Deuteronomic source A and a
Deuteronomic source B [81.26 ff]. This pre-Deuteronomic
source is a part of the Yahwistic historical work [81.95 ff]. In
both sources the originally independent tradition of the
crossing of the Jordan found acceptance. At the center point of
this tradition was the erecting of tablets on the holy ground at
Gilgal, which form critical analysis has shown to be a
cultic-ritual narrative [81.120 ff]. This tradition can be traced
through many steps of transmission to the oldest level of
tradition. It is reconstructed in the following way: Priests, as
the bearers of the ark of the "Lord of the whole land," preceded
the people into the Jordan. As the priests stood in the Jordan,
the water of the Jordan disappeared. The priests remained in
the middle of the Jordan. In the Jordan the instruction was
given to select twelve men—one man from each tribe of Israel.
The command was given to the twelve men to pick up twelve
stones. During that time the priests remained standing in the
Jordan. After the stones were picked up, the priests lead the
people out of the Jordan. As the people came up out of the
Jordan, the water of the Jordan returned to its place. The
twelve stones were erected in Gilgal. The erection of the stones
was joined to a cultic (etiological) teaching recitation in which
the significance of the stones was related to the crossing of the
Jordan. The narrative gave a central place to the twelve holy
stones of Gilgal, and after their erection, they were counted as
part of the inventory of this holy place. As the main actors in the
tradition, the priests stood clearly in the foreground. Thus the

main thread of the narrative was described moreover as a result of the action of these priests. Very early the preservers of the tradition of the Jordan crossing were, therefore, priests at the holy place of Gilgal. As I have shown in another place [81.104 ff], form critical and tradition critical sources indicate that this tradition had its setting in the Matzoth festivity at the holy place in Gilgal. The consequence of the reconstruction (81.167 ff) of this feast can be expressed in the following way.[2]

2. Festival Events During the Matzoth Feast at Gilgal

The prelude to the Matzoth Festival was the pilgrimage of bearing the ark from Shittim (Tell el-Hammam) in east Jordan to Gilgal. The procession would leave Shittim and make an 8 kilometers-journey westward to the fords of the Jordan near El Maghtas. Before passing through the Jordan, a cultic act of cleansing took place. On the following day the fording of the Jordan[3] occurred as the priests with the ark went ahead of the people. In the middle of the Jordan a cultic act took place, which was related to the stones that stood at the holy place at Gilgal. In this act, the place where the priests stood signified the original location of the Gilgal stones. At this place there was thus produced an etiological teaching concerning the origin of the holy stones. From there the procession moved on to the west bank of the Jordan and 8 kilometers farther to Gilgal (Khirbet El-Mefjir). As a conclusion to the Jordan procession there followed a cultic-etiological teaching recitation in which the stones served as a symbol of the event of the Jordan crossing. Following this cultic act the seven-day festival of Matzoth was celebrated (Josh. 5:10-12). The grain in the unleavened bread, as well as the grain that was roasted, represented the produce of the land, which was taken after Palestine was entered. A circumcision festival was also

connected to the Matzoth rites (Josh. 5:2-5, 8b). In the later
Israelitic tradition in Exodus 12:43 ff the rule was that only the
circumcised could participate in the Passover or Matzoth
festivity. Such a connection between the Matzoth Festival and
circumcision must have existed very early at Gilgal. During the
seven days of the Matzoth Festival a procession around the
ruins at Jericho (Josh. 6) took place [81.191 ff]. In the ritual the
procession was divided into the order of armed men, priests
with trumpets, the ark, and the people. On the seventh day the
fall of the walls was cultically dramatized by the blowing of
trumpets and war cries. In Joshua 5:10-12 strong emphasis was
placed on the taking of the land in the Matzoth Festival at
Gilgal. Accordingly a reenactment of the taking of the land
occurred during this festival in the crossing of the Jordan and
the seven-day procession around Jericho.

The Matzoth Festival at Gilgal, therefore, was composed
of two great cultic acts: (1) the procession of the ark from Shittim
to Gilgal with central emphasis being placed on the crossing of
the Jordan, (2) the festival of circumcision that was connected in
the Matzoth Festival to the holy place of Gilgal. The
seven-day-long festival involved a march around the ruins of
Jericho with the ark. The marching around Jericho also casts
some light on the meaning of the cultic procession through the
Jordan. In the Matzoth Festival there was a cultic realization of
the taking of the west Jordan land by Israel. This interpretation
is also supported by the connection of the Matzoth dough with
the first produce of the land of culture.

The cultic taking of the land was accomplished by Israel as
a closed union of twelve tribes. Great weight was placed at
Gilgal on the number—twelve tribes as an expression of the
wholeness of Israel. There the twelve holy stones, which even
in pre-Israelitic time belonged to the inventory at Gilgal, were
rooted in the calendar number twelve and related to the tribes.
The taking of the west Jordan land by a closed union of twelve
tribes was not a historical event. Rather, it was a process that

took place over many centuries by the occupation of the land by nomadic tribes. In Joshua 3–6, therefore, there is no historical record of any action involving the taking of the land by Israel or any mention of a collection of etiological tales. Instead, we have narratives that were deduced from repeated cultic events and then, as they were told, stylistically modified into a unique historical event. If the narrative tradition was derived from a cultic event, then we can postpone the question concerning the relationship of the cultic event and the historical situation realized in it. Thus, the question becomes even more important as we see the procession of the ark around Jericho as a means of enacting the destruction of the city. The Late Bronze Age city of Jericho was sparsely inhabited and had no fortified positions. If no historical conquering of the Canaanite city by the Israelites took place, then the question must be asked concerning the reason for the construction depicted in this ritual. Fortunately, this is not our only source in reconstructing the cultic ritual of the Matzoth Festival, but beyond that we have available in this context an edited covenant tradition. Both in source A (Josh. 4:7, 9) and source B (Josh. 3:3, 6, 8) as well as our present basic tradition, "the ark of the Lord of the whole land" is viewed as the "ark of the covenant." This is also true in the pre-Deuteronomic traditions [81.199 ff]. If an ark of the covenant was stationed at Gilgal, then the question must be asked if the celebration of the covenant had a place in the framework of the Matzoth Festival at this holy place. A comparative analysis of Exodus 34:9a, 10, 11b, 12-26 (J) with Exodus 20:23; 23:12, 14-19, 20-23 (E); 33:2; Judges 2:1-5; 13 and Deuteronomy 7 shows that these traditions, transmitted in various degrees of arrangement, were dependent on a common basic tradition, which had its setting in the Matzoth Festival at Gilgal.

At the center point of this covenant tradition [81.202 ff] stood a decalogue of cultic commands. The oldest reconstructable step of this covenant tradition, in outline form, can be worded as follows:

Take heed and listen to my voice, for my name is in your midst. If you listen to my voice and do all that I say, then I will become an enemy of your enemies and oppress your oppressors. Behold I make a covenant (with you). Before all your people I will do marvels, such as have not been wrought in all the earth or in any nation; and all the people among whom you are shall see the ways of the Lord; when my messenger goes before you and leads you into the land, he will drive out before you the Amorites, the Canaanites, the Hittites, the Perizzites, the Hivites, and the Jebusites.

I: You shall not make a covenant with the inhabitants of the land lest it become a snare in the midst of you.

II: You shall not worship another god, for Yahweh is a jealous God.

III: You shall not make yourself any graven images.

IV: You shall keep the Matzoth Festival at firmly appointed times in the month Abib, for in the new moon of Abib you came out from Egypt.

V: You shall not see my face with empty hands.

VI: You shall do your work in six days and celebrate the seventh.

VII: And you shall observe the feast of weeks, the first fruits of harvest, and the feast of ingathering at the end of the year.

VIII: You shall not offer the blood of my sacrifice with leaven.

IX: And the fat of my festival offering shall not be left until morning.

X: You shall not boil a kid in its mother's milk.

And I will bless your bread and water, and I will root out sickness from your midst. None shall miscarry or be barren in your land; I will fulfill the number of your days. I will send my terror before you and will throw into confusion all the people against whom you shall come, and I will make all your enemies turn their backs to you.

The cultic Decalogue is characterized by the first commandment, the commandment concerning the making of covenants, as well as the following injunction against worshiping other gods or making graven images. The latter injunction originally concerned making images of foreign gods. The connection of covenant and command in Yahweh's covenant with Israel implied a separation of Israel from the inhabitants of the land. The introductory paraenesis joins the observance of the commands to the expulsion and destruction of the people of the land: "If you listen to my voice and do all that I say, then I will become an enemy of your enemies and oppress your oppressors."

The covenant viewed as Yahweh's common dealing with Israel found its expression in the expulsion of the inhabitants of the land. "I make a covenant with you."

This statement is continued and carried out in the following promise. "Before all your people, I will do marvels, such as have not been wrought in all the earth or in any nation. . . . When my messenger goes before you and leads you into the land, he will drive out before you the Amorites, the Canaanites, the Hittites, the Perizzites, the Hivites, and the Jebusites."

This connection is also true for the promise emerging from the cultic legend. "I will throw into confusion all the people against whom you shall come, and let all your enemies flee from you and I will send confusion before you until the remaining ones and the hidden ones are destroyed." The covenant consequently was directed to the situation of the taking of the land that was enacted in the Matzoth Festival at Gilgal. The cultic legend confirms the presumed anti-Canaanite tendency in this festival that was expressed in the conquering procession around Jericho.

3. The Experience of Reality in the Matzoth Festival

The taking of the land by nomadic tribes was a process that extended over many centuries. It was a complicated endeavor by which the nomadic tribes in the culture of Palestine united themselves into the union of the tribes of Israel. It took place chiefly in the course of events that led, first of all, to the occupation of the thinly settled mountain regions of Palestine. Only in the premonarchical period of the Judges do we see military actions against Canaanite cities such as Early Iron Age Bethel (Judg. 1: 22-26) and Ai (Josh. 8). This action took place during a phase of land acquisition and extension. Still, the middle Palestinian tribes, despite some success, experienced the fact that they were not equal to the Canaanites who were highly armed with iron weapons. This premonarchical situation is evident in Joshua 17:14-18. The inhabitants of the house of Joseph complained to Joshua that their place of dwelling in the mountains was not satisfactory. A move into the fruitful plains was also not possible. "The hill country is not enough for us; yet all the Canaanites who dwell in the plain have chariots of iron, both those in Bethshean and its villages and those in the valley of Jezreel."

This condition accounts for the negative view of the possession of the land in Judges 1:21, 27-33, 35. The Canaanite and Philistine cities were located in a position that made it difficult for the tribes of Israel to take them. This state of power continued on through the period of the Judges and was only basically changed under David. He succeeded in bringing the city state enclaves into his kingdom.

The ritual of the taking of the land in the Matzoth Festival at Gilgal did not mirror the situation of the historical peaceful taking of the land by nomadic small herdsmen who, as they changed pastures, increasingly tended to occupy the land. Much more we are directed back to the time of the Judges before the existence of the state, a period in which the occupying tribes reached out to the fertile plains of Palestine and increasingly became involved in military conflict with the inhabitants of the land. A good example is found in the Deborah narrative in Judges 4-5, which reflects that kind of situation.

There the conflict over the possession of the land had its
beginning. It was only at the beginning of the period of the
Judges that Israel began to mix with the Canaanites. This
association in turn produced strife concerning the legitimacy of
the possession of the land and the allied subject of religious
identity.

The situation set forth in the traditions of Joshua 17 and
Judges 1 shows the inferiority of the middle Palestinian tribes
and stands in stark contrast with the taking of the land ritual at
the Matzoth Festival in Gilgal. In that ritual there was an
enactment of the miraculous destruction of the fortified
Canaanite city of Jericho that brought the festival to a
conclusion. Excavations in Jericho by K. M. Kenyon after
World War II demonstrated that Jericho was only sparsely
populated during the Late Bronze Age and was deserted
around 1325 B.C., a hundred years before the settlement of the
Exodus group in middle Palestine. Jericho also had no
fortification at that time [57.256 ff]. The last great wall of
Jericho dates from the Middle Bronze Age and was destroyed in
1550 B.C. by Egyptian troops. The ritual involving the
conquering of Jericho in the Matzoth Festival at Gilgal,
therefore, had no relation to a concrete historical remembrance
of a taking of the land by Israel. Therefore, the development of
the ritual must be rooted in the experience of the premonarchical period, created in an attempt to deal with the
experiences of that time. How can it happen that in a time that
predates the threatened inferiority of Israel over against the
inhabitants of the land a cult ritual was developed, which
depicted a miraculous conquering of a Canaanite city?

It is evident that a wide difference existed between the ritual
and the political reality of the time in which it was
embedded. Thus, the motif of the twelve tribes of Israel was
firmly anchored in the ritual: from the tribes twelve men
were chosen as representatives (Josh. 3:12; 4:2,4) and carried

the twelve stone tablets. These twelve tablets which belonged to the holy inventory at Gilgal likewise were related to the twelve tribes (Josh. 4:5, 8). A union of twelve tribes of Israel in this ritual enacted the taking of the land. This motif had no relationship to a historical event in which the land was actually taken. Even in the time of the Judges there was no united band of twelve tribes which carried on military action. At that time the tribe of Judah did not belong to Israel.[4] Judah's position can be explained in reference to the geographical-political situation of the premonarchical period. The large number of Canaanite and Philistine city states could not be conquered. To these belonged the chain of city states along the coastal plain reaching from Gezer up into the Ephraim mountains to Gibeon, including Zorah, Aijalon, Jerusalem and the cities of the Gibeonite tetrapolis, Chephira, Beeroth, and Kirjath-jearim. These cities divided Judah from the other tribes of Israel and prevented a direct access to the north. Thus there is much to be said for the fact that Saul was the first to join Judah to the remaining tribes [81.322 ff].

In view of this political situation in Gilgal, prior to the establishment of the state, how could a ritual have been developed involving the taking of the land by a united twelve tribes of Israel? The premonarchical claiming of the land was marked by strife with the inhabitants over the possession of the land. This period was also marked by a collision of various religious identities. This historical situation was resolved through the cult. Two factors were at work in this; each directly involved Yahweh, for Israel had been constituted through a covenant with him. Yahweh gave them land and fruitfulness and promised to drive out the inhabitants. The activity of Yahweh took place in the realm of a historically experienced reality in that it was placed back into an ideal beginning situation of the taking of the land of the west Jordan by a united band of twelve tribes under a covenant that promised the possession of the land. This, of course, was a situation that did not happen historically. The festival concluded in the driving out of the inhabitants from their fortified cities. This concept of the taking of the land, which was rooted in the Matzoth ritual at Gilgal, was produced by projecting back into the past dimension, the period of the taking of the land, the basic questions being asked in the historical present of the premonarchical period of the Judges. The same covenant that established the unity of Israel during the Matzoth Festival also separated it from the local inhabitants. According to the promises of the covenant, the local tribes would be destroyed and driven out. These promises were celebrated through an enactment of the fall of Jericho and became firmly established through an annual repetition of the rites as well as being recorded in a cultic Decalogue.

The provocation brought about by the conquering of the land evoked questions and debates with the local inhabitants. The problem was finally resolved through a religious festival in which Yahweh, the God of Israel, was portrayed as guiding Israel into the land. It is he who announces that he will drive out the inhabitants of the land and bless the land if Israel is obedient. In the Matzoth ritual of the conquering of Jericho, Israel celebrated the political reality of Yahweh's promise to drive out and destroy her enemies. This was a process that had already begun to happen. The fruitfulness of the land that was attributed to Yahweh was celebrated in the Matzoth ritual. Roasted grain was brought forward, representing the first produce of the land. In the Matzoth Festival the Israelite farmer celebrated the gift of the land at Gilgal, the holy place, as well as the blessing of the harvest that was rooted in Israel's taking of the land. It was also seen as Yahweh's *heilsgeschichtliche* gift of the land. The blessing of the fruitfulness of the land, celebrated in the Matzoth Festival, was not rooted in a primitive, distant, mythological event that had to be realized cultic, but rather in a historical event, the taking of the land as Yahweh's gift.

The importance of the taking of the land in the Matzoth

ritual indicates a very vital aspect of the whole Matzoth Festival. The religious identity of Yahweh worship was assured during the period of strife with the religion of the inhabitants of the land. Certainly the fruitfulness of the land was thereby traced back to Yahweh and not to Baal. In the cultic Decalogue the constitution of the people as a unity in the covenant by Yahweh was tied to a sharp separation from the religion of the inhabitants of the land. The land was a gift of the covenant, and Israel would finally take possession of it if she held only to Yahweh and refused any possible contact with the inhabitants of the land and their gods. The present difficulties of tribes situated in middle Palestine in the premonarchical period of the Judges were resolved through an enactment of an ideal primitive situation of the taking of the land.

Finally, the same can be said of the motif of the taking of the land by the united twelve tribes of Israel, an idea which was rooted in the festival. During the time that the taking of the land was celebrated cultically in this form at Gilgal, the tribe of Judah remained separated geographically, politically, and cultically from the other northern and central Palestinian tribes. How did it happen that the cult at Gilgal developed the idea that the southern tribe was included in the union of tribes called Israel? The first clue comes from the geographical situation of Gilgal in the southern part of the Jordanian rift. A direct union of Judah with the central Palestinian tribes was prevented by a zone of Canaanite cities. The only connection possible between Judah and the other tribes was through the Jordan Valley. The holy place at Gilgal was thus a famous cultic meeting place for Judah and the remaining tribes. The geographical situation of Gilgal contributed to the fact that exactly at this holy place the idea of twelve tribes could come into being—a union that included Judah.

However, what historical relationships could have produced the fact that one spoke of twelve tribes of Israel at Gilgal even before that political unity was realized? The tribe of Judah (from Leah) was certainly not a complete stranger since in the premonarchical period other central and north Palestinian tribes stemming from Leah were united with tribes originating with Rachel. The connection between Judah and the other tribes of Leah in the north was lost because of the wandering of the tribes of Rachel and the catastrophe that was experienced earlier by the central Palestinian tribes of Leah (Gen. 34; 35:21-22; 49:3 ff). The connecting Leah tribes of central Palestine lost their significance. Judah had also belonged to the community of the Leah tribes and was isolated by the catastrophe that had happened to those tribes of central Palestine. Their isolation was strengthened by the Canaanite circle of cities, which blocked any link between Judah and the Rachel tribes who had wandered into the area of the declining Leah tribes in central Palestine. After the union between the tribes of Leah and Rachel had been effected in the north, Judah led a solitary existence in the south. Like the remaining Leah tribes, Judah was a worshiper of Yahweh. For this reason it is evident that, whenever the geographical situation allowed, communication took place between Judah and the ethnically related tribes of the house of Joseph who also worshiped Yahweh. Judah was thus drawn into the cult. This happened in the Jordan River Valley at the holy place, Gilgal, where the first step was taken of drawing Judah out of its isolation, which had taken place after the catastrophe to the central Palestinian Leah tribes and the migration of the Rachel group. A characteristic of the Gilgal cult that might have attracted the Judeans in the south, who were ethnically and religiously related, was the strong consciousness of being different from the Canaanite inhabitants. This consciousness was rooted in the promise of "driving them out" and in the commands of the covenant. Thus there came into being at the holy place in Gilgal an idea of a union of twelve tribes, which included, to be sure, the tribe of Judah. The fact that twelve Matzoth stones stood at the holy place of Gilgal (taken over from the Canaanites) must have played a role. So it is now clear how the Matzoth stones whose number twelve originated with the months of the calendar were applied to the twelve tribes in the religion of Israel.

They could experience at this holy place in the Jordan River Valley the fact that the tribe of Judah, which worshiped Yahweh and was ethnically related to them, was not a part of Israel and stood apart. This isolation was overcome in the cult where Judah was recognized as a part of Israel. Judah was drawn into the ideal original situation of the cultic taking of the land and shared in the covenant with Yahweh as a part of the unity of Israel. In a deep dimension of reality, Judah was already a part of Israel,[5] even if that cultic claim would only later be politically realized. Many pressing experiences of the present premonarchical period were resolved in this cult: (1) the military strife with the Canaanite inhabitants; (2) the question of religious identity in the conflict with the religion of the inhabitants; (3) the debate concerning the legitimacy of the ownership of the land by the local inhabitants; (4) finally, the realization that the tribe of Judah, ethnically related and worshiping Yahweh, stood isolated and was not a part of the union of tribes. These experiences were resolved in a cultic dramatic way by enacting the original situation of an ideal taking of the land by Israel. This cultic taking of the land did not portray an actual historical event of the past. This process involved tribes of the premonarchical period of the Judges projecting answers to their questions concerning occupying foreign land into a past dimension characterized by taking of the land.

Let us shed some light on that process. A present problem situation received an ideal solution in the dimension of the past. The solution of the problem was reached for the present through an ideal event of the past. Thus it becomes clear how Israel arrived at the concept of being a unified group of tribes that marched victoriously under Yahweh's leadership into the land of culture. The ideal event in the past that had no actual relationship to the real process of taking the land was transcended through a symbolical enactment in the present of the festival. It opened to that present a future dimension of salvation. The concept of a unified band of twelve tribes who, as the people of Yahweh, were lords of the land was a utopian idea of the Israelites of the premonarchical period. The promise of destruction and expulsion of the enemy, which was expressed cultically in the ritual conquering of Jericho, was a way of transcending the everyday experience in which the tribes of Israel were unable to take the numerous city states of the local inhabitants. They were also blocked from the fruitful areas of the Palestinian plain. The taking of the land by a unified band of twelve tribes constituted by Yahweh also transcended the everyday experience in which Judah, a tribe of Leah, was isolated from the rest of the tribes. This separation was caused by a barrier zone of Canaanite cities. The enactment of an ideal past, a utopia pushed into the past, became the foundation for a future of salvation. Yahwch would give more and more of the land into the hand of Israel even as he did at Jericho, a fact that was celebrated in the festival. Yahweh would constitute Israel as a union of twelve tribes by including Judah. The twelve stones set up at Gilgal, the holy place, already symbolized that hope. The utopian dimension, which was rooted in the original situation of the cultic taking of the land, was enacted in the festival event and continued on into the future and transcended everyday experience.

4. "Cult as Drama" in the Matzoth Festival at Gilgal

However, how could it happen—even if ideally—that tribes occupying the land in the premonarchical period would view the taking of the land as a past event whose consequences are realized now and extend on into the future. Here one must consider the function of cultic dramatic actions, such as the procession of the ark through the Jordan and around Jericho. "The new creation happens in the cult in that the new that shall become is expressed in rituals. The holy must 'take place' and must be 'portrayed' in order for reality to happen," says S. Mowinckel [76.73]. The dramatic actions in the cult were not just symbolical dealings reflecting reality, but they also created the reality presented. A festival, therefore, was not just an acted-out drama, a play, but rather a real drama that produced powerful reality. If the Israelite took part in the cultic drama, he thus received a share of the coming reality inherent in it and was drawn into it. In the Matzoth Festival, therefore, the encompassing of the ruins of Jericho by the ark procession represented a cultic conquering of the city as part of the taking of the land. This cultic enactment made the conquering become present again. In this way, however, the salvific power contained in the act became real in the present. It demonstrated the power of Yahweh in leading Israel in victory over a Canaanite city. When this power became reality in the annual festival, there streamed from this cultic reality salvific power upon the everyday experience of the tribes around Gilgal. Israel shared in the festival as a unified band of twelve tribes. This fact was symbolized through the procession of the community and the twelve stones. In a cultic dramatic way it took the land by marching through the Jordan. The eating of the Matzah bread symbolized the fruitfulness of the land. In a cultic procession around Jericho, Israel drove out the inhabitants of the land. The salvific power of this cultic act had the power to shape everyday reality in which strife existed throughout the land. Events portrayed in the festival pertaining to a salvific past had the ability of mitigating the threatening and oppressive aspects of everyday experience by delineating a salvific horizon that transcended the present and went on into the future.

5. Historical-Political Effects of the Festival Event

We are confronted with a further aspect of the festival event in ancient Israel. If the festival had the function of

resolving problems from everyday experience through a ritual
fulfillment of a salvific past, then one can ask how this cultic
event influenced the concrete forms of everyday political and
historical experience.

> In the premonarchical period the prohibition against treaties
> which was recited at the Matzoth Festival of Gilgal had an
> effect on the Gibeonites (Josh. 9). Indeed, that tribe since
> very early times had lived in a neighborly, peaceful relation
> with the Benjamites who had taken some of the land. In the
> course of the premonarchical period the prohibition against
> treaties was expanded and put in operation. Thus, one must
> explain why in spite of this prohibition a treaty was made
> with the Gibeonite tetrapolis, which was traced back
> through a list of the inhabitants of Gibeon [81.317 ff].

Under Saul, Gilgal attained a high point of political import. In
this holy place Saul received his crown (I Sam. 11:15). Saul's
political activity was strongly influenced by Gilgal. During his
reign the tribe of Judah was joined to the other tribes
[81.322 ff], and there a motif from the Matzoth Festival at
Gilgal was brought into actual political reality. To that end Saul
tried to turn the promises of destruction and expulsion into
political reality in that he determined to root out the
inhabitants of Gibeon and Beeroth [84.67 f]. Tradition found in
II Samuel 21:1-14 points to that fact. David, while hungry,
learned through an oracle that Saul and his house had blood
guilt on its hands, because he had put to death the Gibeonites.
As expiation, the survivors of the massacre demanded the death
of Saul's sons. "The man (Saul) who consumed us and planned
to destroy us, so that we should have no place in all the territory
of Israel" (II Sam. 21:5). Saul's action had as its purpose to
destroy all the inhabitants of Gibeon. Second Samuel 4:2-3
shows that it was not a matter of a single action. As a
consequence, the Canaanite inhabitants of Beeroth fled from
Saul to Gittaim. Gibeon and Beeroth were two of the cities with

which the Benjamites had concluded a treaty relationship. However, as Joshua 9 makes clear, they had become scandalized for doing so because of the prohibition against such treaties. Saul wished to annul the vasal relationship and carry out the treaty prohibition, as well as the expulsion and destruction promises of the Matzoth Festival at Gilgal. He desired to bring all of these into political reality. Saul's action in II Samuel 21:2 was also interpreted in that light. "Although the Gibeonites had taken an oath with Saul, Saul sought to slay them in his zeal for the people of Israel and Judah." The realization of the promise of destruction was anchored in the very beginning days of Saul's reign, for in the latter years we must remember that he had very little political-military freedom, in view of the threat from the Philistines and the tragic end of his reign.

The Israelite cult of the premonarchical times demonstrated through the Matzoth Festival at Gilgal how Yahweh had overcome the problems of concrete historical-political experience. They did this by projecting their present problems into the dimension of an ideal past or salvation history. Through this process new political-historical realities were set forth that transcended the present realities.

III. Reflection: From Fear of Magic to the Birth of Hope in the Yahweh Festival

We have followed stations of the way that lead from the cultic resolution in the Passover of problems, which the pre-Israelitic seminomads met in changing pasture, to the Matzoth Festival which was rooted in premonarchical Israel at the holy place, Gilgal. The nomadic Passover was determined by the efforts of the nomads to ward off demonic powers through an apotropaic blood ritual. They feared that demonic powers would bring them bad luck as they broke camp for new grazing grounds. This bad luck needed to be diverted. The fact that bad luck might be turned into a salvific force through some process did not enter their minds. Thus, every year in the spring the destroyer needed to be warded off. The basic theme of the nomadic Passover was the fear of the powers who needed to be kept from their destructive work but who, at the same time, could not be defeated. This implied theme in the Passover celebration was basically changed as the Passover in Israel became interpreted from the point of view of Yahweh. For the tribes who had settled down it served as a time of remembrance of the salvific rescue of those fleeing Egypt by the God of Sinai. In this marvelous event the historical power of Yahweh became visible in his ability to rescue them out of the hand of the Egyptian power. Yahweh reached into history and turned it into the salvation of Israel. From the cultic portrayal of this salvation-history event in the Passover of the Israelitic tribes in the land of culture came the knowledge that Yahweh would once again, as in the Exodus, reach into their present and effect salvation. The fear involved in protecting themselves from demonic power gave way to joy and to the certainty of the salvation that Yahweh would give. From this certainty, rooted in the Exodus experience of Yahweh's power in history, a festival was built involving the taking of the land celebrated in central Palestine in the Matzoth Feast at the holy place of Gilgal. In this festival the experience of political threats and questioning of religious identity was addressed and resolved. The cultic rite of taking the land was a reality that was contrasted with Yahweh's unifying of the twelve tribes. This contrasting reality was celebrated in the festival and became the foundation for the fact that Yahweh would increasingly carry out his salvific intent for Israel.

H. Cox [19.14 ff] has worked out the connection of the time dimensions of the past and future in reference to the festive present: "Since the festival breaks through the routine and opens man to the past, it widens his experience and reduces his provincialism. Phantasy opens doors, which empirical calculation overlooks" [19.21]. If it is true that modern experience with tradition opens up the meaning of the past, then one can also say that experiences determined by the present can be widened through festive enactments of past events, and in the process new possibilities for the formation of the future in everyday life can be realized. In Israel's experience of festival, these time dimensions were bound even closer together. Israel, which had now settled on the land, interpreted the political-social situation in the land of culture over against the experience of Yahweh's salvific historical power that had been demonstrated in the Exodus experience. Here challenges and experiences were projected into the past dimension of an ideal taking of the land. The experience of the present was disrupted, and the festival became a foundation for Yahweh's determining everyday reality with his salvation. The past dimension, which is interpreted from the point of present-tense problems, not only affords possible choices for the formation of the future over against present-tense ones but also demonstrates that only by going back to the past can there be the possibility of a salvific future. The everyday experience of the future will make real that which has been established in history and enacted cultically in the present. The limitations of this way of dealing with reality and overcoming it are not to be overlooked. The future is open only for that which is already established in the past and ritually celebrated in the cultic event. Accordingly, the future becomes only a peripheral theme of the Matzoth Festival in the sense of a time dimension, such as expressed in the promises. It was present only in an implied way in the cultic enactment of salvation history that possessed the power to transcend the present. Another limitation of this dealing with reality is to be recognized in the fact that the idea of salvation did not go very far beyond the ethnic and religious borders of Israel. Much more, the concepts of Israel's salvation crystalized around the central themes of expulsion and destruction of the inhabitants of the land.

The journey from the nomadic forms of comprehending reality to the Matzoth Festival at Gilgal in the premonarchical period was a very long one for Israel. But how much longer would it take to reach an understanding of salvation that would encompass all men and a festival celebrated that would articulate every creature's sigh?

IV. The Fall Festival

Saul's politics, which had as a goal the destruction of the Canaanites, came to an end in his defeat in the battle against the Philistines at Gilboa (I Sam. 31). Out of the confusion following the death of Saul, David emerged as the new ruler of Israel. He was first of all anointed as king by the tribe of Judah (II Sam. 2:1-4). Only after the death of Abner was he recognized by the other tribes. David was consequently king in a personal union over the house of Judah and over Israel, which included the other ten tribes of central and northern Palestine.

At first David reigned from Hebron, but this city lay too far in the southern fringe of his kingdom to please the central and northern tribes and, thus, could not continue to serve as the capital city. Faced with that situation, David made a very clever move. He did not move his residence from Hebron in Judea to an Israelite area, but rather attacked the Canaanite city of Jerusalem that was inhabited by the Jebusites (II Sam.

5:6-10). It lay in the territory between Judah and the remaining tribes of Israel and was a neutral territory inhabited by Canaanites. After being conquered, it passed over into the personal possession of David, and he now became king of Jerusalem. In the conquering of Jerusalem, David did not involve the soldiers of Israel's tribes, but allowed the city to be conquered by his own men. In contrast to Saul who had been influenced by Gilgal, David did not kill the Canaanites in Jerusalem. Everything points to the fact that he allowed the Canaanite inhabitants, around twenty-five hundred (113.33 ff) in number, to live in the city without reprisals or limitations and made them his subjects. A correspondingly tolerant attitude on David's part can be observed in reference to other inhabitants of his monarchy and its city states. As a consequence of David's victory over the Philistines (II Sam. 5:17-25), David took possession of the Canaanite cities of the Palestinian plain that had been controlled previously by the Philistines [3.49 ff]. These political developments became evident in the description of the boundaries given in II Samuel 24:5-7 and the list of the districts and overseers in I Kings 4:7-19. The Canaanite territories were not added to the Israelite tribes, but rather preserved their own political and social independence under the supremacy of Jerusalem [80.178]. David's tolerant religious politics with the goal of integration stood in contrast to the politics that had a goal of the destruction and expulsion of the Canaanite inhabitants.[6] Thus, David named a Jebusite priest, Zadok, to be priest of Yahweh alongside of Abiathar [102.8]. In the course of building the temple, David's successor, Solomon, followed in his father's footsteps by allowing an altar to be set up in the Canaanite mold. This was precisely forbidden in a law, dating back into the premonarchical period, concerning altars (Exod. 20:24-26). This development can be explained only by observing the influence of the Jebusite-Canaanite culture tradition on the religion of Yahweh after the conquering of the city by David

[18.135]. Thus, the mythical motifs and rituals of the Jebusite cult in Jerusalem were integrated into the Yahweh religion of David's city. Only from the point of view of this Canaanite influence can the form of the festival events in Jerusalem be understood. We now turn to the Canaanite religion of Jerusalem of the pre-Israelite period.

1. Canaanite Religion in Pre-Davidic Jerusalem

The Canaanite religion of Jebusite Jerusalem cannot be investigated in a direct fashion, since we do not possess Jebusite traditions. We are directed to subtle conclusions out of Old Testament traditions of preexilic Jerusalem in comparison with traditions of Canaanite religion of the Syrian-Palestinian realm, especially the Ugaritic [102, *passim*]. Above all, we have in Genesis 14:18-20 an old fragment of tradition that reaches on into the time of David and demonstrates an essential characteristic of Jebusite religion.

> Melchizedek, however, the King of Salem brought out bread and wine; he was a priest of El, the Elyon, and he blessed him and spoke: "Blessed is Abraham of El, the Elyon, the creator of heaven and earth, and blessed is El, the Elyon, who gave your enemy into your hand." And he gave him a tenth of all.

This old Jerusalem tradition, dating from the early period of the kings, was influenced by the motif of El, the Elyon, the one who had delivered the enemy into the hand of Abraham. This tradition was written back into Genesis 14 in a rather late literary tradition concerning a battle of the kings.

From a history of traditions' point of view Genesis 14:18-20 is independent of this narrative but yet is to be interpreted from it. Thus, the Melchizedek tradition concerned itself with a time before the taking of Jerusalem by David, an epoch of the patriarch Abraham, at a time distant to the perspective of the early period of the kings. This epoch was ruled by Melchizedek the priest-king of Canaanite-Jebusite Jerusalem and honored El, the Elyon, as the highest one, the creator of heaven and earth. The identification of El with Elyon points to a displacement of the text since originally El and Elyon were contrasting gods. The process of joining these two divinities who were equal in their functions was already at work in Jebusite Jerusalem [102.161 f]. This process found its conclusion in the identification of El and Elyon with Yahweh after the conquering of Jerusalem by David. The peculiarities and functions of these gods were carried over to Yahweh and consequently outlined in Genesis 14:18-20.

Three dimensions of Jebusite religion in Jerusalem are addressed in Genesis 14:18-20: the creation of heaven and earth, the destruction of the enemy, and the fruitfulness of the land. Let us now turn to the last of the three motifs of Canaanite religion, the gift of the fruitfulness of the land.

This theme is addressed in the motif of the priest of El, Melchizedek, bringing out bread and wine, which as Ugaritic parallels show [102.151, note 12] points to a cultic meal. In Jebusite Jerusalem the fertility of the land was attributed to the gods, El, *Salem* ("peace") and *Saedaeq*[7] ("salvation"). Thus, Psalm 85:13-14 indicates a Jebusite concept that is visible even after its transferal to Yahweh.

(El) bestows his blessing, and our earth gives its fruit,
Saedaeq goes before him and *Salem* in the traces of his step.

In this tradition Yahweh has been placed back in the position of El. The original Jebusite cultic tradition told of a procession of the gods from which came the blessing of the fertility of the earth. This blessing, which produced fertility, was traced back to El but was actually mediated through the lower gods *Salem* and *Saedaeq*. The fertility that El manifested was the part of his being that could be expressed in the form of a bull. In addition to that, El of Jerusalem demonstrated traits of the earlier Baal worship, which was seldom practiced in Jerusalem. The gift of fertility finally was based on El's creation of the world.

The creation myth of the Jerusalem El joined two contrasting motif complexes in the history of religions. They reflect the joining of a remote God with a divinity of vegetation. Thus El was viewed as the one who had created the firmament of the earth, who held back the primitive ocean and separated earth and heaven. He had also stretched out the heavens over the earth that had been stamped flat as a disc. Over against this creation myth of the remote God with its separation of the primitive sea, firmament, heaven, and earth stood the concept that the creation of the world was a result of a battle against the chaos monster represented by the chaotic sea and mentioned in the Old Testament by the names Rahab, Tannin, or Leviathan. El drove away the power of chaos who then turned and fought. In the course of their flight, El shattered the head of the chaos dragon. With this victory the sea, which threatened the world of created beings, was put back into its limits. The creation and preservation of the world in that mythological primitive time and the present exist together in this complex of conceptions.

The cosmic dimension is essential to both views of creation. That of the remote God rests directly in the concept of the course of creation. It is indirectly implied in the concept of creation connected to the battle with chaos. During the battle the mountains wobble, and it is questionable if the created world will be submerged in the assault of the sea or will retain an area of salvific life set off from chaos. If through creation the chaos powers were defeated in a cosmic dimension, then the *destruction of the enemy people* who attack the mountain of God represents a corresponding theme in the political dimension.

Oh, the thunder of many peoples, they thunder like the thundering of the sea. Oh, the roar of nations, they roar like the roaring of many waters. Though (El) he will rebuke them, and they will flee far away, chased like chaff on the mountain before the wind and whirling dust before the storm at evening time, behold, terror! Before morning, they are no more (Isa. 17:12-14).

The people who storm the mountain of God (a motif widely in evidence in the Jerusalem tradition) remain amazingly pale in their political-historical contours. Earlier they had appeared as "a shapeless entity without a political profile—a surging mass" [89.II, 163]. Any actual military action within this tradition is very doubtful and the whole weight of the tradition rests on a miraculous destruction of the enemy before the mountain of God. Thus, the subject is not just the fact that El destroyed a definite enemy before Jerusalem but that the condition of salvation created by the destruction of the chaos powers is also to be predicated in the political dimension. This political function of the pre-Israelite-Jebusite El of Jerusalem is reflected in the tradition of Genesis 14:18-20. There El is blessed as the God who "delivers your enemies into your hands."[8]

The destruction of the enemies was closely connected with the mountain of God in Jerusalem. Here, before this mountain, the enemy people were destroyed. This connection was rooted in the fact that the mountain of God was El's dwelling place. It was the central point of the world (Ezek. 38:12) to which heaven and earth were bound to one another.[9] Thus, the El of Jerusalem could be set forth as living in heaven and on the mountain of God.

> You said in your heart, I will ascend to heaven; above the stars of El I will set up my dwelling place; I will set my throne on the mountain of God, on top of the Zaphon: I will ascend above the heights of the clouds, I will make myself like Elyon. (Isa. 14:13)

Zion was identified with Zaphon, the Canaanite mountain. If El lived on the mountain of God, then his kingdom was tied to it!

"His holy mountain, beautiful in elevation, is the joy of all the
earth. Mount Zion, the peak of Zaphon is the city of a great king"
(Ps. 48:2). Thus, the mountain of God could be held as the
foundation of the house of God and the support of the divine
throne.

The kingdom of El of Jerusalem brought together the
universal functions of creation and salvific preservation of the
world in the cosmic and political dimension as expressed in the
battle of the chaos dragon and the people. As the general in
God's pantheon of Jerusalem, El was the kingly judge of the
gods and the earth. He carried out salvific justice into the social
order and came to the help of the poor, the pitiful, the widows,
and the orphans. El was judge over the people, setting forth the
rights of Jerusalem against its enemies. And finally El judged as
king over the gods. This combination of themes bringing salvific
order on earth and judgment among the gods is seen quite
clearly in Psalm 82, which can be traced back to a Canaanite
origin before being attributed to Yahweh.

> God has taken his place in the Council of El,
> in the midst of the gods he holds judgment.
> How long will you judge unjustly
> and show partiality to the wicked?
> Speak justice to the poor and the fatherless,
> maintain the right of the afflicted and the destitute.
> Rescue the weak and the needy;
> deliver them from the hand of the wicked!
> They have neither knowledge nor understanding,
> they walk about in dullness;
> all the foundations of the earth are shaken.
> I say, "You are gods, sons of Elyon, all of you;
> nevertheless, you shall die like men and fall like any prince.
> Arise, O God, judge the earth!
> For to you belong all the nations."

We have sketched a picture of the Canaanite-Jebusite religion
of pre-Israelitic Jerusalem. The contrast with the comprehen-

sion of reality in the Yahweh religion of the premonarchical period at Gilgal is evident. Salvation in its cosmic-universal and political-social dimensions was not rooted in an experience of salvation history of a saving God but rather was based on an act of God in the primitive mythological dimension. The fight against the chaos dragon did not take place in the realm of actual historical experience, but it was an event that was rooted in the distant mythological dimension of primitive time. The cultic enactment of this mythical reality transcended the encountered experience of reality. Its salvific effects could be experienced. Even the theme of the battle of the people could not be traced back to a concrete historical event of the history of Jerusalem, for it transcended every actual political experience in its miraculous destruction of the enemy. It was experienceable only in its effects, the security of the city of God. Even so, the fertility of nature and establishment of Jerusalem's well-being over against the other nations was not rooted in a *heilgeschichtliche* intervention of El into history but rather was rooted in the dimension of mythological reality that went beyond history. The power of El to delineate a salvific area of creation over against the chaos of the primitive mythical dimension, which transcended every experience of reality, gave the certainty that El could carry out blessed life in the experience of reality in the cosmic, political, and social dimensions. If the action of El was founded in the mystical dimension, then the universality of his rule and action could be understood as extending from the mountain of God in Jerusalem unto the whole created world. He made heaven and earth; he was lord over the nations; he was lord over the gods. In this universal sphere of rule, Jerusalem was considered to be the seat of God and the midpoint of heaven and earth.

In Gilgal Yahweh was spoken of in other ways. Yahweh's salvific work for Israel was not rooted in a mythical reality that transcended historical experience but rather rested in the experience of his reaching into the present political-social history, be it in the Exodus from Egypt or the oppression in the premonarchical land of culture. If the powerful acts of Yahweh that created blessedness were not rooted in mythical reality but rather historical experience, then one can understand his actions being limited to Israel. The rule of Yahweh over the nations was not apparent, only his rule over the people of Israel against the other nations. The people of Israel were constituted in the covenant with Yahweh. The action of Yahweh had as its goal to secure a place for his people in the land of culture. Foreign people were important only as the inhabitants of the land whom God would destroy and from whom Israel should keep its distance, because these people served foreign gods. In the Gilgal of the premonarchical period it was not a matter of dominion over other peoples and gods but rather a call to separate themselves from these gods and peoples, because they would be destroyed by Yahweh.

The *religionsgeschichtliche* differences between early Israelite-Jebusite-El religion in Jerusalem and the premonarchical Israelite-Yahweh religion in Gilgal is clear. As a result, the question is asked, How was the Yahweh religion developed under Canaanite influence after the conquering of Jerusalem by David? How was it consolidated anew in the festivals in terms of understanding and dealing with reality?

2. A History of Research Concerning the Festival of Throne Ascension

Since the reconstruction of the Fall Festival in Jerusalem belongs to the most disputed areas of Old Testament research of the last fifty years, we cannot help but briefly sketch a history of this investigation.

The Psalms stand as our best available source for the reconstruction of the Jerusalem cultic event. We owe a debt to the Norwegian Old Testament scholar S. Mowinckel [75 II, *passim*] who established that the greatest number of the Psalms had their setting in the cultic activity in the temple in Jerusalem and should be interpreted from that point. Therefore, they were not witnesses to individual pious prayers but rather official cult events in the temple. The combination of the results of the history-of-religions school with those of form-critical methodology and motifs of northern European research in religion led Mowinckel to his view of the Jerusalem cult. This cult was not shaped by motifs of the Christian dogmatic tradition, but rather was guided by an attempt to apply categories adopted from ancient pre-Christian religions to the phenomenon of the Israelite festival. For Mowinckel, a cult is a festival, lifted up from the mundane experience, a holy time through which everyday life is made possible. In the cult the blessing of Yahweh was carried over to the life of the individual and the community. The relationship between people and God was rooted in the festival. Beyond that, however, the Israelite society also was constituted by Yahweh in the festival. The universal rule of God over the whole world of creation was brought to expression in Yahweh's ascending of the throne. This action expressed the change of fortune that took place in the festival of Yahweh for the good of all in the coming year in all areas of experience. This hope for the future was founded on a new creation of the world effected by the ascension to the throne and with it a new order of relationships. The people believed that the strength of the creation was used up in the course of the year. Consequently, all of life must be constantly renewed and ordered and must be made secure against chaos if it was to avoid becoming chaos again. This new creation was worked out in different concrete acts: Yahweh would destroy the enemies of Israel, judge the nations, carry out Israel's right, and establish a kingdom of peace. Nature would overflow with fertility, and Israelite society would live in justice. The king would be responsible for the outsider in society. In what concrete way would this bestowal of blessing and the new creation of the world that results from it be realized? Here

Mowinckel's thesis of "cult as drama" (see chapter 2) is introduced in which he establishes that cultic actions are not to be interpreted symbolically but rather as graphic realities. Therefore, if in the cult, chaos, powers, and enemy nations were dramatically destroyed, then they were really destroyed. This fact became obvious in the course of the year. Through sharing in the cultic drama in the festival events at the Jerusalem temple, the Israelite actually received a part of God's new created reality in the world and was drawn into it.

At the climactic point of the Fall Festival, the ascension to the throne was presented cultically and dramatically through the procession of the ark. Therefore, as the Israelite shared in the procession of the ark which symbolized the ascension of the throne by Yahweh and the covenant celebration, he experienced the reality of blessing that was connected with it and that was expressed more concretely in the ecstasy of the festival. Since he shared in the ritual of the destruction of the enemies advancing on Jerusalem, he also participated in the reality of the kingdom of peace brought about by the defeat of the enemy.

Mowinckel sets forth the following reconstruction of the festival of throne ascension in the temple at Jerusalem:

> Yahweh comes, he reveals himself and is greeted by the jubilation of nature and the pious. He takes up the fight against the enemy—the actual enemies and rivals of Israel—or he summons them before his throne of judgment; the Gentiles and their gods are judged, "shamed." In any case the full reality will be brought "ideally" into focus in the course of the year. This will take place if Israel does not thwart its salvation by its sins, as had happened earlier. In triumph, Yahweh makes his way to his temple on Zion, ascends his throne and is honored by his subjects. He determines the fate of the coming time; he concludes a new covenant with his people while guaranteeing them all salvation if they keep his commands and walk "uprightly"

according to his will. He judges the world, i.e., he puts it in an order which corresponds to the "righteousness rooted" in the covenant. This fact of faith is cultically celebrated through the great procession of the king (II Sam. 6). The ark is led up in a procession to Zion. The entrance of Yahweh is made dramatically visible through symbols and holy actions, through the holy "drama" of the cultic procession. The king, the priests, and the entire people are there and share in the cultic dance. Prophetic voices are heard. Offerings are brought; hymns are sung; prayers are prayed; the horns resound; the holy temple music rings out. The ecstatic festival joy possesses the participants and they become certain of the reality of the merciful arrival of Yahweh in this spiritual experience [75 III, 31]

It is hardly an exaggeration to conclude that the subsequent Old Testament research is to be understood in its essential development up to the present-day as a reaction to Mowinckel's interpretation of the Israelite cult as the chief institution of Israelite religion.

In the English and north European direction of research in "ritual patternism" [68.460 ff] one sees a *religionsgeschicht-liche* question concerning the primitive attitude of man over against his world. This school of research, principally represented by S. H. Hooke, G. Widengren, and I. Engnell, overemphasizes the influence on Israelite religion of the ancient oriental history of religions and thereby reduces considerably its scientific worth. The circle around Hooke projects a cult scheme which determined the whole fertile crescent from the land of the two rivers to Egypt. In the midst of this stood a dying and rising divinity whose fate determined the change from the dry season to the rainy season or reduction of life to possibility of life. In the midpoint stood therefore a universal renewal of life which was expressed in a holy wedding which was carried out by an earthly royal couple. In the northern school, centered around Widengren and Engnell, the divine function of the king is still disputed.

Mowinckel, who turned energetically against this direction of research, at no time connected the idea of Yahweh as a dying God to the festival of the throne ascension. Much more for Mowinckel, the ascension to the throne is a confirming renewal of the rule of Yahweh. It is quite another thing in the school of research which follows him: here Yahweh annually loses his rule—represented in the cultic defeat of the king—in order then to gain it anew in the triumph of the ascension of the throne and to confirm it through a holy marriage. However, in the Old Testament there is no convincing proof of a dying Yahweh or a wifely escort in the holy marriage. Thus, this further development of Mowinckel's thought is not convincing.

There are also German scholars who raise objections to Mowinckel's proposals. Thus, the influences of the modern word-of-God theology should not be overlooked if it is true that the Israelite cult must be protected from being interpreted as an *ex opere operato* active event. This systematic theological motif was clothed in an exegetical thesis strategic for research. Over against Mowinckel, the peculiarity of the Israelite cult is worked out in the fact that worship is formulated in contrast to the surrounding world of Israel. Within the circle of this problem the significant contrast between faith and religion in the framework of dialectical theology plays an important role. In Old Testament exegesis it was expressed as a differentiation of the faith of Israel from the religion of its neighbors, and likewise it was a challenge to be extolled in the cultic question of Israel's peculiarity. In this context belongs above all the work of A. Weiser, G. von Rad, H. J. Kraus, and C. Westermann.

A. Weiser [109.22 ff; 108.513 ff] replaces the throne ascension with the renewal of the covenant as the center of the Fall Festival. The festival consisted of two great cultic acts: the *actio Dei*, the act and word of God which were expressed in theophany, proclamation of God's name, and the revelation of

Yahweh's essence. In reference to their content, they were cultic recapitulations of salvation history as well as proclamations of God's will in the form of the giving of commandments on the basis of which the renewal of the covenant took place. Finally, judgment was actualized in the ritual of blessing and cursing. The *reactio hominum* stood over against that judgment and composed the true confession of the community—the holiness and self-purification of the cultic community. At the center of the festival of covenant renewal might have stood the word event of the proclamation of the salvation deeds of Yahweh and his commandments.

In support of this "protestant" interpretation of the Jerusalem cult H. J. Kraus [67, LXIV ff] has gone a bit farther in that he also interprets the cultic theophany as a proclamation event. A cultic-dramatic enactment of the Yahweh theophany would contradict his inavailability so that the theophany event may represent an earlier description of the charismatic proclamation of cultic prophecy. Instead of a covenant renewal festival Kraus opts for a preexilic "royal Zion festival" in which there may have been an enactment of the selection of Zion, as well as the selection of David and his dynasty in the promise of Nathan, by an ark procession [67.879 ff]. While Kraus still reckons with an actual word revelation event in the cult, G. von Rad [89, I. 366 ff] sees in the Psalms, rooted in the cult, the essential "answer of Israel" to the revelation that had occurred in Yahweh's salvation deeds in history. Israel did not remain speechless in regard to these salvation deeds (the salvation history from Abraham to David). Israel not only endeavored anew to make them present in historical vessels, but also spoke quite personally to Yahweh, asked questions of him, and made lament to him for its sorrows. For Yahweh had chosen his people not as a silent object of his historical will, but rather as a partner in dialogue [89, I. 366-67]. Over against Mowinckel's thesis of a dramatic cult, which effected salvation at the Jerusalem temple, von Rad sets forth [90.9 ff] a reconstruction of the great cultic endeavors that stressed the unique Israelite rites at the holy sites of Gilgal and Shechem. The influence of the surrounding area is not as apparent there as in the cult of Jerusalem in the premonarchical period of Israel. During the Feast of Weeks at Gilgal the credo of Yahweh's salvation history from the patriarchs to the taking of the land stood at the central point. At Shechem the celebration of the covenant took place at the Feast of Tabernacles, which emphasized the word event of paraenesis and proclamation of the law.

G. Westermann [110.112] dissolves the connection between Gattung and its social location which had been so necessary for form critical analysis since Gunkel. He interprets the setting of the Psalms over against the petitions and praise which take place in word from man to God. The question concerning the function and meaning of the institution of the cult is finally removed from view.

The dispute of German language Old Testament research with Mowinckel has been centered in no small measure in the systematic-theological questioning of the present. Thus, Mowinckel's central question for the understanding of the Israelite cult in reference to its function in concrete life within the context of Israelite society was pushed extensively into the background. By expressly asking this question of Old Testament exegesis, Mowinckel contributed his most unforgettable service.

3. Was a Throne Ascension Festival Celebrated in Preexilic Jerusalem? (An Analysis of Psalm 47)

The difficulty of reconstructing the Fall Festival in preexilic Jerusalem is due to the fact that we possess no description of the course of the festival or its ritual that belongs in this context. We must, therefore, direct our attention to the Psalms, which we assume were arranged around the Fall Festival, and conclude that the course of this festival became the setting of the Psalms in question. A confirmation of this fact may be attained through a careful *religionsgeschichtliche* comparison with the festivals of the surrounding world. However, the exegesis of the Psalms should not be prejudiced in any way in this regard. It is obvious that this procedure has a circular argument that produces a forced conclusion. As a result, the selection of the textual foundation is decisive for the reconstruction of the festival and cannot be guided by a previous idea of the festival. We attempt in the following to reduce as far as possible the uncertainty produced by the text. We start not with a maximum number of texts but rather a minimum number—in fact, just Psalm 47, which was central among the psalms of throne ascension. Thereby, we will try to avoid an exegesis that would read into the psalm a previous view of the festival. Consequently, we shall start with the language level and emphasize linguistic structure.

Psalm 47 To the choirmaster, from the Sons of Karah. A Psalm.[10]

v. 1 Clap your hands, all peoples,
Shout to Yahweh with loud songs of joy!

v. 2 For Yahweh, Elyon, is terrible,
a great king over all the earth.

v. 3 He subdued peoples under us,
and nations under our feet.

v. 4 He chose our heritage for us,
the pride of Jacob, whom he loves—selah.

v. 5 *Yahweh has gone up with a shout,*
Yahweh with the shout of a trumpet

v. 6 Sing praises to Yahweh, sing praises!
Sing praises to our king, sing praises!

v. 7 For Yahweh is the king of all the earth;
sing praises with a psalm.

v. 8 *Yahweh reigns over the nations;*
Yahweh sits on his holy throne.

v. 9 *The princes of the peoples gather as the people of*
the God of Abraham; for the shields of the earth
belong to Yahweh; *he is highly exalted!*

In order to emphasize the linguistic structure of the psalm, it is necessary to give attention in the following to the inflection of the verbs in the framework of the parallel units. An overview demonstrates the following results:

Half Verse a	Half verse b	Structure line		
v. 1 Imperative	Imperative	a	a	
v. 2 Nominative				
Sentence	Nominative Sentence	b	b	
+kî (for)				
v. 3 Imperfect	(Imperfect)	c	c	
v. 4 Imperfect	(Imperfect)	c	c	
v. 5 *Perfect*	*(Perfect)*	d		d
v. 6 Imperative	Imperative	a	a	
v. 7 Nominative				
Sentence		b/(a)		
+kî (for)	Imperative	b/(a)	(a)h	
v. 8 *Perfect*	*Perfect*	d		d
v. 9 *Perfect*	Nominative Sentence	d(b)	(b)	d
Perfect	+kî (for)	d		d

This overview demonstrates that the psalm is composed of two structural entities placed one after another in verses 1-5 and verses 6-9. They have the following basic structure:

1. Exhortation in the *imperative*
2. Grounding of the exhortation in a *nominative sentence*
3. From these are deduced sayings in the *imperfect*
4. *Statements using the perfect tense*
   The structure thus has two poles: the exhortation in the *imperative* as an introduction and the statements in the *perfect* as the conclusion. The nominative sentences have the function of furnishing a foundation for the exhortations.

   a. Clap your hands, all peoples,
      Shout to Yahweh with loud songs of joy!

b. For Yahweh, Elyon, is terrible,
   a great king over all the earth.

This connection between the imperatives and the nominative sentence becomes even clearer in the second structure, because here the basic nominative sentence is surrounded by the imperative.

a. Sing praises to Yahweh, sing praises!
   Sing praises to our king, sing praises!
b. For Yahweh is the king of all the earth;
a. Sing praises with a psalm.

The basic nominative sentence is interpreted in the first structural entity by the statements in the *imperfect*. In the Psalms the imperfect has extensively the function of reporting an action that is dependent and is not important in itself [73.176]. This function is seen in Psalm 47. The statements in the imperfect in verses 3-4:

c. He subdued peoples under us,
   and nations under our feet, he chose our heritage
   for us, the pride of Jacob whom he loves.
   (introduce the basic nominative sentence)
b. Yahweh, the Elyon, is terrible, a great king over all the
   earth.

Just for this reason, the peoples ought to praise Elyon. Thus, next to exhortation (a) supported by units (b) and (c), the perfect tense statements (d) take on their own weight. This significance is further underlined by the fact that the structural entities point to and find their goal in the perfect tense structure elements. Thus, the first structural unit finds its high point and goal in the statement in verse 5:

d. Yahweh has gone up with a shout,
   Yahweh with the shout of a trumpet.

The assertion that Yahweh goes up has an equivalent in the second structural unit in the climactic statement of verses 8–9a):

> d. Yahweh reigns over the nations;
> Yahweh sits on his holy throne.
> The princes of the peoples gather as the
> people of the God of Abraham.

The weight of the perfect tense in the framework of the entire psalm is further underlined by the fact that the second structural entity is dominated by four statements in the perfect. The third of these is strengthened even more by a foundational nominative sentence. A decision concerning the interpretation of the psalm especially in reference to its setting is therefore dependent on the understanding of these structural elements in verses 5, 8, 9.

In verse 5, the first structural unit has as its goal the description of an act of Yahweh (going up: '$al\breve{a}h$) in a perfect tense statement. Probably emanating from it is a characteristic action for the perfect-tense statements in verse 8 (he has become "king": $mal\breve{a}k$; he "sits": $y\breve{a}s\breve{a}b$), which serve as the goal of the second structural unit.

The imperative exhorts them in jubilation to become a part of the event, the ascending of Yahweh, his ascension to the throne, and to share in this event with praises. The basis for this lies in the power of Yahweh as Elyon and king, who has already revealed himself in the past in that he had placed the nations under the feet of Israel and chose Israel for an inheritance. The perfect-tense elements in verses 5, 8, and 9 point to actual events in which one is to participate according to the exhortation of the imperative. The nominative sentence bases this exhortation on the uniqueness of Yahweh whose proof—as the imperfect-tense statement will show—has been obvious in the past.

This structure of the psalm, therefore, demonstrates that

at the center point of the cultic act is to be found the *throne ascension*. That theme blends well with the basic motif of this psalm; the sound of the trumpet and shouts of jubilation belong to the enthronement of earthly kings (II Sam. 15:10; II Kings 9:13), as well as the clapping of the hands (II Kings 11:12). Finally, the cry of proclamation[11] "_____ has become king"[12] is also found in II Samuel 15:10 and II Kings 9:13. From the linguistic structure and motif of the psalm one can conclude that it had its setting in the framework of an ascension to the throne.

Thereby, the question is raised concerning what was enacted in the act of ascending the throne. The relationship between verses 5 and 8 is also decisive for this question. The ascension of Yahweh as seen over against II Samuel 6; I Kings 8; and Psalm 132 is to be interpreted in reference to the carrying up of the ark in the procession to the temple. With the carrying up of the ark to Zion (verse 5) Yahweh ascended his throne and took over the rule, verse 8. In verse 9 the ascension to the throne is tied to the assembly of the princes of the people to Abraham's God. Corresponding to this event, the power of Yahweh as Elyon in verse 3 is based on his success in the political-historical dimension in the subduing of the nations. In view of that, it is obvious that one should see in the carrying up of the ark the actualization of an event in the historical dimension, namely David's bringing the ark to Jerusalem as symbolizing the taking of God's mountain by Yahweh. This connection is confirmed by Psalm 132. In the throne ascension, it is not a matter of the realization of the mystical event of creation, but a matter of a historical event. Mowinckel's reconstruction of the throne ascension emphasized too much the creation and new creation in a cosmic-mythological dimension while the cultic concrete salvation history experience of Israel was too little valued. He brought in the analogy of the Babylonian New Year's Feast, which afforded the closest parallels for scholars of the 1920s. The procession of the ark to Zion was viewed as bringing in Yahweh to Jerusalem, who is then enthroned over the ark. Jerusalem had been conquered earlier by David. If Yahweh were understood as being enthroned invisibly over the ark, then the bringing in of the ark symbolized Yahweh's taking possession of Zion. The procession of the ark in the Fall Festival brought the realization of that hope. That means, however, that Canaanite universalistic theological terms, such as creation of the world, the kingship of the godhead over the world and over the nations, were connected to Zion, which was then viewed as the mountain of God, and to Yahweh. His ascension to the throne was traced back to the historical event of bringing in the ark—that is, the taking possession of his divine place. In addition, a comparison of Psalm 47 and Psalm 93:96-99 shows that the throne ascension brought together a historical realization of the bringing in of the ark with a mythical-universal taking over of rule.

4. The Festival Event and Experience of Reality in the Fall Festival

A reconstruction of the results produced by individual cultic acts in the Jerusalem Fall Festival of the preexilic period remain hypothetical because of the reasons already stated; though it is clear that the ascension to the throne was only one cultic act, though a central one, among others. Psalm 47:132; II Samuel 6; and I Kings 8 all indicate that the prelude of the festival was the procession of the ark to the temple by the participants.

The narrative of the ark (I Sam. 4–6; II Sam. 6) gives us a view of this procession. At the appearance of the ark, the people broke into cries of jubilation; the trumpets resounded; the people danced ecstatically before the ark; zithers, harps, timbals, bells, and cymbals clanged together. The music burst forth; Yahweh was enthroned supremely and invisibly over the ark; the joy, the jubilation, and the dance were the direct effects of the nearness of God. Yahweh was the immediate source of the joy, the dance, and the ecstasy. Around him was an intensified reality of blessing, peace, salvation—the reason for the jubilation:

> Yahweh has gone up with a shout,
> Yahweh with the sound of a trumpet,
> Sing praises to Yahweh, sing praises!
> Sing praises to our King, sing praises! (Ps. 47:5-6)

Psalm 48:12-13*b* points to the fact that a part of the procession of the ark included a march around the walls of Jerusalem:

> Walk around Zion, go round about her,
> Count her towers!
> Consider her ramparts,
> Go through her citadels.

The course of the festival becomes more clear when the procession of the community reached the temple area. Here there took place an opening-of-the-gates liturgy (Ps. 15:24) in which the theme of the congregation's loyalty was stressed as the condition for opening the gates. The lead group in the ark procession lifted up their voices before the gates:

> Lift up your heads, O gates.
> And be lifted up, O ancient doors!
> That the King of glory may come in. (Ps. 24:7, 9)

A priest answered from the closed temple area, "Who is the King of glory?" (Ps. 24:8, 10). Those in the procession outside the gates answered:

> Yahweh, strong and mighty!
> Yahweh, mighty in battle! (Ps. 24:8)

and

> Yahweh, Lord of hosts—
> He is the King of glory. (Ps. 24:10)

This scene of cultic antiphonal music before the gates of the temple area was in the form of a liturgy concerning the conditions of community loyalty needed for entering the temple area:

> Who shall ascend the hill of the Yahweh?
> And who shall stand in his holy place?
> He who has clean hands and a pure heart
> Who does not lift up his soul to what is false
> And does not swear deceitfully.
> He will receive a blessing from Yahweh
> And vindication from the God of his salvation.
> Such is the generation of those who seek Yahweh
> Who seek the face of the God of Jacob. (Ps. 24:3-6)

In contrast, therefore, to the New Testament understanding of cultic justification, preexilic Israel thought of only "a justification of the righteous." In the festival event only the one who has shown loyalty to the community in the course of the past year could seek the power of blessing residing in the cult at the holy place of Jerusalem. Community loyalty was a presupposition of this blessing.

With joy the procession of the community reached the outer courts of the temple. The song of praise was sounded:

> Make a joyful noise to Yahweh,
> All the lands!
> Serve Yahweh with gladness!
> Come into his presence with singing!
> Know that the Yahweh is God!
> It is he who has made us, and we are his;
> We are his people, and the sheep of his pasture.
> Enter his gates with thanksgiving,
> And his courts with praise.
> Give thanks to him, bless his name! (Ps. 100:1-4.
>   Compare Psalms 95:1-7; 99:4; 118:19-20.)

Psalm 118:19-27 points to the fact that the liturgy of entering the gates involved a dance around the horns of the altar in the outer courts of the temple.

The high point of the festival involved *the bringing of the ark into the most holy part of the temple,* which was accompanied by the shout of proclamation, *"Yahweh has become King."*

Psalms 50 and 81 [81.300 ff, note 2] demonstrate that the Fall Festival was terminated with the *concluding of the covenant,*[13] a sacrifice, and proclamation of the commandments.

There is something new here that goes beyond the taking of the land ritual in evidence at the Matzoth Festival at Gilgal. It is the universal significance of salvation that is related to the whole creation in the Fall Festival at Jerusalem. In taking possession of the divine mountain by Yahweh, salvation breaks through to the whole creation, for Yahweh, the Elyon, is the creator of the world:

> Yahweh has become King, robed in majesty;
> Yahweh is robed, he is girded with strength,
> Yea, the world is established; it shall never be moved;
> Your throne is established from of old;
> You are from everlasting, God. (Ps. 93:1–2)

The historical event of the transporting of the ark by David as a sign of Yahweh's taking possession of the divine mountain can be traced back to Psalm 47 and the throne ascension. In the perspective of Jerusalem, this event actualized the mythical-universal dimension of El's or Elyon's creation. Salvation's historical and mythical dimensions flow into one another. In the act of ascending the throne, a fact of salvation history is actualized. However, in taking over the universal mythology of the Canaanite religion, rooted in the divine mountain, this event of salvation history has a dimension that encompasses all of creation and thus negates the old premonarchical view that salvation history was effective only for Israel. The cardinal point of Yahweh's salvation activity remains an event of salvation history and is not sought in a primitive mythical event as in the Canaanite religion. Israel, itself, remained loyal in Jerusalem, but the limitation placed on Yahweh's work among the nations was broken and now his acts were for the whole world. Thus, the claim inherent in the Fall Festival of Jerusalem was that creation takes place, was safeguarded, and was renewed against the chaos monster. This claim was cultically portrayed in David's bringing in of the ark, which in turn symbolized Yahweh's taking possession of the divine mountain. This mythical dimension had its origin in the framework of Jebusite-Canaanite religion.

> The floods have lifted up, Yahweh,
> The floods have lifted up their voice,
> The floods lift up their roaring.
> Mightier than the thunders of many waters,
> Mightier than the waves of the sea.
> Almighty is Yahweh on high. (Ps. 93:3–4)

The concept "people of the world" was now related to a dimension of salvation which was directed to the whole world.

> Ascribe to Yahweh, O families of the people;
> Ascribe to Yahweh glory and strength;
> Ascribe to Yahweh the glory due his name;
> Bring an offering and come into his courts;
> Worship Yahweh in holy array;
> Tremble before him, all the earth!
> Say among the nations, "The Lord reigns!"
> Yea, the world is established, it shall never be moved.
> He will judge the people with equity. (Ps. 96:7-10)

The Fall Festival had a salvific function for all the people, because Yahweh, as a creator God, was Lord. The Jerusalem temple was viewed, therefore, not only as a gathering point for pilgrims in Israel but also for all the nations. These nations, as Israel, worshiped Yahweh and recognized him as Lord of the world. Thus, Psalm 47 concludes with the assertion:

> The princes of the peoples gather as
> The people of the God of Abraham.
> For the shields of the earth belong to
> Yahweh. He is highly exalted.

This psalm reflects not only the universal claim of the Jerusalem cult, which was rooted in the mythical dimension of the Fall Festival, but also the actual political experience of the great kingdom of David and Solomon. It is no longer just a matter of separation as was found at Gilgal where Israel set itself apart from the inhabitants by the acceptance of the covenant and looked toward their being driven out. Here it is a matter of the recognition of the Jerusalem temple and its God, Yahweh, by foreign people. The foreigners are no longer absolute enemies of Yahweh and his people, but rather only the ones who do not give Jerusalem its due and will not recognize Yahweh as the highest God.

Through the assimilation of Canaanite mythological terms, there comes into being a consciousness of the function and significance of Yahweh, of his people, of his temple in Jerusalem, of the world, and of all nations. This would also become the foundation of Christianity's universality.

In the festival of throne ascension mankind and nature respond to the salvation that is going out from Jerusalem over the whole world.

Yahweh has made known his salvation,
He has revealed his vindication in the sight of the nations.
He has remembered his steadfast love and faithfulness
To the house of Israel.
All the ends of the earth have seen the salvation of our God.

Make a joyful noise to Yahweh all the world
Break forth into joyous song and sing praises!
Sing praises to Yahweh with the lyre,
With the lyre and the sound of melody!
With trumpets and the sound of the horn
Make a joyful noise before the king, Yahweh!
Let the sea roar, and all that fills it!
The world and those who dwell in it!
Let the floods clap their hands;
Let the hills sing for joy together before Yahweh
For he comes to rule the earth. He will judge the
world with righteousness and the people with equity. (Ps. 98:2-9)

Joy and praise in the Jerusalem Fall Festival were more than just an expression of emotion for cult participants; they were rather a ritualistic reaction to the salvation realized in the festival for mankind and nature. From a Canaanite point of view, this ritualistic joy was related to a divine ascension to the throne [46.98 ff]. From an Israelite perspective of salvation history it was related to the enactment of bringing in the ark (Ps. 47:2 ff).[14]

The basis of the jubilation, therefore, was not in mythical-primitive events, but rather in the immediate gift of Yahweh who had reached into the historical experience of reality and from Mt. Zion bestowed his salvific power. The realization of this salvation-history event of throne ascension viewed as Yahweh's taking of Zion as his divine seat made real the rule of Yahweh over the world. Before God, salvation and blessing flowed from the festival into the world, which received this blessing in the festival community through festive praising of an enhanced life ('simhā) and by jubilant worship (terúā).

Yahweh's festive ascension of the throne brought salvific power in three dimensions. In nature a fruitful new life appeared; in the greater world of the nations Yahweh judged and destroyed his enemies; and in the social dimension the deed-result association (see note 15) brought misfortune to the

evildoers and salvation to those loyal to the community. A
sphere of community loyalty was thus created.

> Yahweh loves those who hate evil,
> He preserves the lives of his saints,
> And he delivers them from the hand of the wicked.
> Light dawns for the righteous
> And joy for the upright in heart.
> Rejoice in Yahweh, O you righteous,
> And give thanks to his holy name! (Ps. 97:10-12)

In this way we have already pursued to some extent the
question concerning the experience of reality realized in this
festival. Since the Jerusalem cult was characterized by the
mythological language of the pre-Israelite-Jebusite cult, one
should not expect an immediate assimilation of the historical-
political experience as in premonarchical Gilgal. Beyond such
religionsgeschichtliche influence we must stress the natural
phenomenon, such as the rhythm of the dry and rainy seasons,
sowing and harvesting, which were in the background of the
experience. The fruitfulness of the land was traced back to
Yahweh and no longer to El as in pre-Israelite Jerusalem. Thus,
Yahweh took over the functions of El by the concrete historical
course of events in which Yahweh of the ark took possession of
the divine mountain after the conquering of Jerusalem.
Through these events he was proven to be the greatest God. In
the premonarchical period, a time characterized by disputes
with the local inhabitants, the pressing problem of religious
agreement at Gilgal led to a sharp separation from the native
peoples. In contrast, at Jerusalem the problems were solved by
absorbing the religion of the local inhabitants and by giving
Yahweh the functions of El.

Festival and experience were not as directly connected in
Jerusalem as in premonarchical Gilgal, because the experience
of reality in the Canaanite religions was oriented to the cycle of
nature and this in turn influenced the Israelite temple cult.

Thus, the Fall Festival of the Israelite period also had a basis in the experience of historical-political reality of the great kingdom of David and Solomon in which the surrounding people and Canaanite city states were subjected to the power of Jerusalem. This subjection included the recognition of Yahweh as Elyon, the highest God. Therefore, we find in Psalm 47 that the princes of the world met together with the people of the God of Abraham. That involved not just the creation of a utopian universalism but a real event in the great kingdom of Solomon. The absorption of foreign people into a great kingdom under Israel's leadership corresponded culturally to the absorption and assimilation of foreign religion into the Yahweh religion. This was accomplished by Yahweh assuming the functions of El and the subjection to him of the other gods in the Jerusalem pantheon. We find a corresponding happening in the religio-political actions of David that were different from those of Saul. In Saul's reign there were evidences of a politics of expulsion and destruction carried out against the city states of the local inhabitants. David strengthened the rule of Israel over Palestine by allowing the Canaanites to retain their ethnic and religous integrity and requiring them only to acknowledge the political supremacy of the Davidic throne in Jerusalem and the supremacy of Yahweh. The changed cultic reality brought about by assimilation corresponded to the changed political reality of a great kingdom integrating all foreign people [84.65 ff].

The festival cults of Gilgal and Jerusalem shared a common structure in that a reality was created by the cult and drama, which transcended the concreteness of everyday life. At Gilgal this abundant reality was expressed in the cultic realization of the possession of the land by the one people, Israel, as the people of Yahweh. At Jerusalem, it was accomplished by imposing Yahweh's universal and blessed rule over the whole world created by him. The execution of this reality, achieved in the cult and drama through concrete acts of everyday reality, was expected to be salvific. Cultic reality would be applied to the formation of everyday reality. However, the decisive fact is that the Old Testament cultic tradition foresaw no problems involved in the carrying out of the festival reality. In contrast the reality produced by the cultic-dramatic rites was viewed as possessing more reality than everyday reality. This everyday reality was deduced from the cultic festival reality and received from it its form as creation and nonchaos.

In this fashion we have come to the heart of our question: reality is produced cultically and dramatically in the festival; salvation comes to pass for Israel and for the whole world. From this festival reality can be deduced concrete forms of political and social reality. Just like nature, everyday reality receives its form in all its dimensions from the cult, its possibility and realization, finally its being, as nonchaos, that is, its nonfictitious being as seen in creation. Cultic-dramatic reality takes place at a holy place by the enactment of an ideal nonmythical history. The uniqueness of Israel resides in the fact that the ideal aspects of her historical past are not discovered through actual past historical events. The ideal nonmythical history transcends the present through cultic-dramatic rites. This picture, created of the salvation-historical past of Israel, cannot be explained or discovered in the actual aspects of Israel's history. This phenomenon has its origin in the cult. At Gilgal it was the original situation of an ideal taking of the land by a united group of Israelite tribes standing under the covenant and promise of Yahweh. At Jerusalem it involved Yahweh's full possession of Zion as the divine mountain and central point of the world, symbolized by bringing in the ark. These are motifs that transcend the present experience of reality through dramatic enactment.

The festival in Israel was the reality of the nearness of God—an intensive reality from which flowed salvation and blessing in the world. In the midst of it all, man began to make joyful, to sing, to praise, and to experience the blessing of God in festive ecstasy. The experience of chaos in nature and society was thus abolished. The nearness of God overcame the estrangement of man from nature, from neighbor, and with himself. Reality was experienced as a whole; man and nature, individual and community, body and reason were all a unity in the experience of the nearness of God.

In the festival God makes possible the world and life; every year the world is constituted in that it is made safe from the on-pressing chaos. The community of the people is grounded in the covenant with Yahweh. Finally, the individual has life only in a qualified sense, because he receives the blessing of God only as a member of the people of God, as a participant in the festival. Everyday reality is, therefore, made possible in the festive reality of the nearness of God.

The challenges of history in nature and society that press into festive reality lead to an expansion of the image of God behind which Christian theology cannot penetrate. The power of God is linked to his love for man. This connection was expressed already in the premonarchical period in the intercession for the oppressed people of God, and at Jerusalem it was given a universal application to the whole world. In the festival God's love for the whole creation was realized powerfully in the destruction of chaos and the penetration of the whole world with his blessing.

5. Myth and Ritual in the Fall Festival at Jerusalem

Here a word should be said concerning the mythical dimension in relationship to the ritual of the preexilic cult in Jerusalem.

The attempts to determine the relationship between myth and ritual have led to many different results. That these myths could have had a cultic setting is not disputed. Thus, the creation epic *Enuma Elish* was read at the Babylonian Fall

Festival. The Ugaritic "Myth of the *Birth of Salim* and *Sahar*" is
furnished with a ritualistic interpretive framework [31.80–81].
The problem arises when one is concerned to determine the
function of myth in the framework of the cult. If, as an
accompanying text, myth is used to explain ritual [Mowinckel
75, II. 19 ff], then would it not bestow an ontological quality on
the cultic dramatic treatment and be seen as an event of God's
reality and thus a unique event bringing the constancy of reality
[Gaster, 30.3, 5, 49]; or is myth only the dramatic script for the
ritual [Baumgartner, 5.88]?

Since the tradition about the rites of the Jerusalem cult are
not available to us, there is no purpose in questioning the
function of mythical expression of reality by reconstructing the
course of the festival. Therefore, we select another way of
approaching the problem that, to be sure, is unavoidable
because of the difficulty of the terrain. In the realm of historical
verification, it is less comprehensible, because we must start
with a mood of mythical reality and from that point address the
question of its possible location in the framework of the Yahweh
religion at Jerusalem.

In myth man attempts to integrate himself into the reality
around him and understand it, for nature is determined by
mythical happenings of gods designed by humans. The gods
live by rules, which correspond to those of human life and thus
can be understood and predicted [77.34 ff]. Thereby the
foreign reality in which man finds himself can be penetrated. If
it is a question, therefore, of the integration of man in his
natural and social environment, then one must link to it the
striving to reduce the risks of reality through mythical
interpretation. Man also strives to make reality more stable in
its form and more foreseeable by mythical interpretation.
Today we cannot help but see the projection of human life
experience in a mythical concept of reality that affords a higher,
more regulated, level of ontologically qualified reality. It will
then determine the experience of reality. But the course of

nature and human events are not only modeled in reference to those of divine-mythical reality, but rather human hopes also in turn influence myth. The complexity of a chaotically experienced reality is reduced to the basic structure of a mythical event, which then sets free the everyday reality contained in it. Thus, there is an expectation of a salvific reduction of chaotic everyday reality and a blessed life is thereby justified. This basic mythical event is viewed in a metahistorical primitive story that emphasizes a beginning event. This process makes it possible to deduce a blessed life in the everyday reality encountered.

Members of the Nordic school [see page 56] have brought into view a Jerusalem cult whose view of reality had been influenced by the mythical form of a rising and dying god. In addition, the examination of the theses drawn from the *religionsgeschichtliche* complexity of ancient oriental religions is faulty and the motif of a dying and rising god (Tammuz) cannot be convincingly proven in the Old Testament tradition. If we place the thoughts drawn from basic religious structures next to a principally mythical interpretation of the Yahweh religion of the Jerusalem cult, we see the following. In two respects the mythical dimension of the Jebusite-Canaanite religion was penetrated by the Yahweh religion. Yahweh was not like the mythical gods, limited by divine events and, thereby, only a member of a higher ontological order. Rather, as the only venerated God, he transcended this order by his power to assimilate and make impotent the other gods. Thus, Yahweh could not be drawn into mythical events, but remained mysterious in his dealing, transcending every foreseen projection. He was not caught up in attempts to stabilize the experience of reality, or to reduce the experience of chaos, or to integrate man into his environment. For Jerusalem another view, which contended that Yahweh's activity was not established in some metahistorical event of the primitive period that determined the unchanging reality of everyday, was basic. Rather Yahweh reached directly into the reality of historical experience and determined this by his historical salvific activity. In a corresponding way, festival joy was viewed as the festival joy of an enriched life that was not affected by a primitive mythical event, but was a joy of praising stemming from Yahweh's action in history.

> Come and see what Yahweh has done;
> He is terrible in his deeds among men.
> He turned the sea into dry land;
> Men passed through the river on foot.
> There did we rejoice in him. (Ps. 66:5-6)

Thus, it is understandable why the myths were replaced by hymns in Israelite Jerusalem. There was no timeless primitive reality present in the preexilic hymns such as one finds in myths, but rather they were oriented to the experience of reality [102.221 ff]. When mythical motifs were taken over into the hymns, they took on the function of expressing the universality and supremacy of the creator God, Yahweh.

V. Revolutionary Changes in the Theology of the Cult After the Destruction of the First Temple

The universal demand made on the nations in the Jerusalem Fall Festival corresponded to the political reality of the great kingdom of David and Solomon. However, what happened to the political experience of reality rooted in the demands of the Fall Festival—a festival that carried out Yahweh's universal rule after the breakup of the great kingdom of Solomon and David? The princes of the peoples no longer gathered themselves at the temple in Jerusalem. On the contrary, in the eighth century the Northern Kingdom experienced defeat by the great power of Assyria, while Judah remained independent. Also increasingly, the order of society broke into pieces. It had rested on the right to the land, which had its origin in the preexilic period. It assured the individual that his land was an inheritance from Yahweh. Instead of this, there was imposed under the influence of Canaanite social order an agrarian economy that brought the land into the hands of a few big landowners, making free Israelites into day laborers, and being landless, they were robbed of their cultic, political, and judicial rights [64.236 ff]. In view of this political-social experience it must be recognized that the kingdom of God was no longer realized festively in the annual cultic ascension of the throne by Yahweh as king, whereby his rule could be carried out increasingly into everyday reality. The reason for this change lay in the disloyalty of the community of Israel. Through the knowledge of Israel's sins, the prophets recognized that the kingdom of God with its accomplishment of Yahweh's salvific rule would be a future greatness, which would introduce a new day, transforming everyday reality. From this tension that existed between a cultic dramatic realization of salvation and an everyday reality marked by sorrow, there came into being eschatological thought, which looked toward the future and expected salvation in it.

The prophetic criticism of the cult was rooted in that kind of situation. If the challenge is raised concerning the possibility of conveying community loyalty in the cultic context, social reality demonstrates, on the other hand, that with the destruction of social order, community loyalty cannot be imposed, even though the ones responsible for it participate in the cult and offer sacrifice. As a result, the prophets replaced the expectation of viewing community loyalty as being achieved in cultic events, with the hope that Yahweh would bring it about through the transformation of everyday reality.

These experiences, which had broken apart cultic reality and everyday reality, making them unbridgeable, were not just fashioned by the prophets after the division of the kingdom or in the eighth century, but also were present in the cultic theology of the Jerusalem temple. There the cult reform of Josiah, which had been influenced both by Deuteronomy and Jewish land Levites, represented an accommodation to the changes that had taken place since the period of David and Solomon. The universality of Yahweh's claim on the whole created world was rooted in David and Solomon's time in the assimilation of Jebusite-theological terms. This unusual claim was reduced to the idea of the unity of "all of Israel" or the people of God in which Yahweh primarily acts. Thus, the thought of the election of Yahweh was stressed while the universal motifs of the Jerusalem Fall Festival were pushed into the background. This reduction corresponded to the resulting separation of Israel from foreign people and their gods. If the temple theology before Josiah was characterized by the assimilation of Canaanite religious motifs, then the worship of one Yahweh included the resulting exclusion of syncretistic elements from the Jerusalem cult. This corresponded to the fact that the claim of Jerusalem of being the central point of the world and the seat of Elyon was reduced to being the central holy place of Israel (Deut. 12). No other place dedicated to Yahweh could stand beside it. If the people of Israel constituted the framework of reference for the actions of Yahweh, then one would expect the geographical setting—the land of culture—to be the central point or dwelling place of the people of God. Yahweh gave the land as a gift of salvation; he destroyed and placed in subjection the nations of the land; he assured a peaceful life in this land and protection from the enemies. The universal motif that Yahweh would judge the people and impose his rule was reduced to insuring the life of Israel in the land of culture.

But the reduction of the universal dimension to a national concern also involved utopian conceptions and futuristic postulates in view of the fall of the Northern Kingdom. Josiah tried politically to bring about this cultic postulate of "the whole Israel" by attacking the area of the former Northern Kingdom (II Kings 23:15; compare 41. 326, 329).

The celebration, rooted in the cosmic and political universality of the ascension to the throne, was reduced to a covenant agreement that had as its goal the constitution of the people of God and their community with Yahweh. The reduction of the universal dimension to a national one also involved an exclusion of syncretistic religious elements. Accordingly such mythical motifs as "the fight against the chaos monster" and "the battle of the nations" fade in importance in the face of motifs of salvation history interpreted for a united people of Israel.

The Northern Kingdom, long exposed to the threats of the Arameans, finally fell to the Assyrians. The experience of this and the Southern Kingdom's loss of independence to Syria brought to an end Josiah's reform. (This can be deduced from the Deuteronomic materials.) This climax can be seen as the reduction of the universal cultic theology of Jerusalem with its concentration on the relationship between Yahweh and Israel and, as a consequence, the tension between cultic reality and everyday experience became correspondingly smaller. The concept that transcended everyday reality was contained and sustained in the thought that all of Israel, as the people of God, was included in the fall of the Northern Kingdom.

In the Deuteronomic material the continuing election of Israel by Yahweh was made concrete in the gift of the land of culture and the quietness of life in the land. This expectation was tied to the demand that Israel must answer Yahweh's love for his people with a love of Yahweh that included the whole heart. This love was expressed concretely in Israel's obedience over against the commands of Yahweh as expressed in the Torah. The paraenesis anchored very broadly in Deuteronomy demonstrated the great concern that Israel might refuse the love of Yahweh and through disobedience lose both the land and peace.

This situation actually took place in the year 587/6 B.C. through the conquering of Jerusalem by the troops of Nebuchadnezzar, the destruction of the city of God, and above all, by the fall of the temple. Israel ceased to exist as an independent state. Was God a powerless God? Was he powerless to secure his mountain, his temple, and his people before the attacking enemies? This doubt, which was reflected in all of its complexity by the prophets of the exile period, could not win the day. Israel did not turn from Yahweh. She recognized much more in the destruction of Jerusalem and the exile of the last Jew that Yahweh was still in her history, even though it was now characterized by her sin. This solution is understandable if seen over against ancient Israel's conception of understanding reality in terms of a "deed-result"[15] relationship. The unhappy course of Israel was rooted in her acts of continual sin. With the destruction of Israel and the consequent exile, the problem of sin became a central motif of Israel's resolution of reality in her religious tradition. This remained a very definitive motif even after her restitution in the postexilic time.

For this reason the theme of sin appeared very much in the foreground in the festival, which was the prime institution for dealing with reality. The cultic event became one for absolving sin. It served the function of breaking the forces of sin and destruction that were caused by the connection of deed to result. It also made it possible for man, who was in a sinful condition, to have life before Yahweh.[16] The liberating jubilation that grew out of the recognition of this new dimension in Yahweh's dealings resounds in Psalm 65:1-4a.

Praise is due to thee,
Yahweh, in Zion;
And to you shall vows be performed,
O you who hears prayer!
To you shall all flesh come on account of sins.
Our sins are stronger than we, however, you forgive them.
Blessed is he whom you choose, and bring near,
    to dwell in your courts.

The expiatory function of the cult was driven to an extreme point in the *priestly document's* utopian idealistic formulation. Most of the cultic practices were reinterpreted around that point [60.45 ff]. All the sacrifices except community sacrifices were reinterpreted as expiatory sacrifices. Motifs of community constitution, thanksgiving, and praise no longer had a place in these activities, which had their origins in other connections and which the Israelites, no longer rightly understood, were interpreted as sin offerings; for example, the mustering of Israel for the payment of taxes (Exod. 30:12 ff) or the service of the Levites (Num. 8:19). This cult conception was embedded in the universal conception of history in the priestly writings, beginning with creation. Yahweh's acts in history moved in a straight line from the beginning of creation to the event at Sinai. They reached their peak in the erection of the tent of meeting and the establishment of the cult that belonged to it. In this way the sins of man were viewed in terms of God turning away on the one side and God turning to men in forgiveness on the other side. In the first place with the establishment of the cult at Sinai, it became possible for man, in spite of his sinfulness, to live in communion with Yahweh. In a dialectical fashion the cult constituted the possibility of man having fellowship with Yahweh. The establishment of the cult laid the foundation for the possibility of sinning, as well as the way for expiation of sins. The point of connection was the understanding of man as a being who was inclined to sin and who had a proclivity to evil. The sorrowful experience of the history of

Israel over against the background of the relationship of deed-result was condensed in an anthropology, which had as its starting point the evil in man. This experience firmly established in anthropology was attached to the cult which then had as its function to make life possible for sinful men before Yahweh.

It is clear that change took place in relationship of the implied anthropology of the festive event to the preexilic Fall Festival in Jerusalem. In the preexilic time man always found his meaning in the festival. Life became possible for man only as being in the area of blessing produced, cultically and dramatically in the festival, a nonchaotic life. Man received life in a qualified salvific sense primarily through the salvation act completed in the cult. There life was constituted and nonchaos came into being. The anthropological dimension was, therefore, transmitted as attainable only through this universal cultic dealing of Yahweh. It was a different matter in the postexilic period where man himself was pushed into the center of the stage. The experience of Israel with Yahweh, shrouded in anthropology, became the basis for the form and function of the cultic event. It was now directly concerned with the possibility of man living before Yahweh. It was no longer mediated as nonchaos[17] in the constitution of the world. God and man in direct confirmation themselves became the themes.

In this context of cultic expiation the thought of substitution was very much alive. Sins could be placed on an animal, which was then killed, instead of a sinful man. Thereby, the priestly writing saw as the center of the expiatory rites the sprinkling of the blood of animals on the altar. Blood was viewed as the seat of life; thus, the life of the animal was offered up for that of the sinner. The evil in man was thus removed as Yahweh opened a way for allowing the effect of the evil deed to fall upon the substituted animal rather than man. In this life, reconciliation with God became possible for man.

VI. Day of Atonement

1. The Ritual Tradition of the Day of Atonement in Leviticus 16

The connection between sin and substitution was very much concentrated in the ritual of the Day of Atonement as transmitted in Leviticus 16. In this tradition the primitive ritual[18] is seen more clearly when it is set in italics in the following translation:

(1) Yahweh spoke to Moses, after the death of the two sons of Aaron, when they drew near before Yahweh and died. (2) And Yahweh spoke to Moses, "Tell Aaron your brother not to come at all times into the holy place within the veil, before the mercy seat which is upon the ark, lest he die; for I will appear in the cloud upon the mercy seat. (3) But thus shall Aaron come into the holy place: with a young bull for an offering and a ram for a burnt offering. (4) He shall put on the holy linen coat, and shall have the linen girdle, and wear the linen turban; these are the holy garments. *He shall bathe his body in water, and then put them on.* (5) And he shall take from the congregation of the people of Israel two male goats for a sin offering, and one ram for a burnt offering. . . . (6) And Aaron shall offer his bullock of the sin offering which is for atonement for himself and his house. (7) *Then he shall take the two goats, and set them before Yahweh* at the door of the tent of meeting. (8) *And Aaron shall cast lots upon the two goats, one lot for Yahweh, the other lot for Azazel.* (9) *And Aaron shall present the goat on which the lot fell for Yahweh, and offer it as a sin offering.* (10) But the goat on which the lot fell for Azazel shall be presented alive before Yahweh to make atonement over it, that it may be sent away into the wilderness to Azazel. (11) Aaron shall present the

bull as a sin offering for himself and shall make atonement for himself and for his house; he shall kill the bull for a sin offering for himself. (12) *And he shall take a censer full of coals of fire from the altar* before Yahweh, and two handfuls of sweet incense beaten small; *and he shall bring it within the veil.* (13) And put the incense on the fire before Yahweh *that the cloud of the incense may cover the mercy seat* which is upon the testimony, lest he die. (14) And he shall take some of the blood of the bull, and sprinkle it with his finger on the front of the mercy seat, and before the mercy seat he shall sprinkle the blood with his finger seven times. (15) *Then he shall kill the goat of the sin offering* which is for the people, *and bring its blood within the veil,* and do with its blood as he did with the blood of the bull, *sprinkling it upon the mercy seat* and before the mercy seat. (16) *Thus he shall make atonement for the holy place, because of the uncleanness of the people of Israel,* and because of their transgressions; all their sins; and so he shall do for the tent of meeting which abides with them in the midst of their uncleannesses. (17) There shall be no man in the tent of meeting when he enters to make atonement in the holy place until he comes out and has made atonement for himself and for his house and for all the assembly of Israel. (18) *Then he shall go out to the altar* which is before Yahweh and make *atonement for it,* and shall take some of the blood of the bull *and of the blood of the goat, and put it on the horns of the altar round about.* (19) And he shall sprinkle some of the blood upon it with his finger seven times, *and cleanse it* and hallow it *from the uncleannesses of the people of Israel.* (20) *And when he has made an end of atoning for the holy place* and the tent of meeting and the altar, *he shall present the live goat.* (21) *And Aaron shall lay both his hands upon the head of the live goat, and confess over him all the iniquities of the people of Israel,* and all their transgressions, all their sins; *and he shall put them upon the head of the goat, and send him away into the wilderness by the hand of a man who is in readiness* . . . . (23) *Then Aaron shall come into the* tent of the meeting *(holy place)* and *shall put off the linen garments* which he put on when he went into the holy place, *and shall leave them there (in the holy place).* (24) *And he shall bathe his body in water* in a holy place, *and put on his garments, and come forth,* and offer his burnt offering and the burnt offering of the people, and make atonement for himself and for the people. (25) And the fat of the sin offering he shall burn upon the altar. (26) And he who lets the goat go to Azazel shall wash his clothes and bathe his body in water, and afterward he may come into camp. (27) And the bull for the sin offering *and the goat for the sin offering,* whose blood was brought in to make atonement in the holy place, *should be carried forth outside the camp; their skin,* and their *flesh shall be burned with fire.* (28) And he who burns them shall wash his clothes and bathe his body in water, and afterward he may come into the camp. (29) And it shall be a statute to you for ever that in the seventh month, on the tenth day of the month, you shall afflict yourselves and shall do no work, either the native or the stranger who sojourns among you. (30) For on this day shall atonement be made for you, to cleanse you; from all your sins you shall be clean before Yahweh. (31) It is a sabbath of solemn rest to you, and you shall afflict yourselves; it is a statute forever. (32) And the priest who is anointed and consecrated as priest in his father's place shall make atonement wearing the holy linen garments. (33) He shall make atonement for the sanctuary, and he shall make atonement for the tent of meeting and for the altar, and he shall make atonement for the priests and for all the people of the assembly. (34) And this shall be an everlasting statute for you, that atonement may be made for the people of Israel once in the year because of all their sins." And Moses did as Yahweh commanded him.

By separating out the rituals of the Day of Atonement that date in the period of oral tradition prior to the priestly writing, it is possible to characterize the tendencies of the *source redaction of the priestly writing* in Leviticus 16. Thus the stress placed on the thought of atonement makes evident its two basic directions. Hence, P expanded the original ritual of atonement for the holy place, which had been made unclean by the

Israelites, to include an atonement for the priest and his family, as well as the people of Israel, through the introduction of a priestly bullock. Within this tendency one also finds the introduction of an atoning burnt offering. The weight that P placed on the priestly atonement is shown in the doubling of the motif in verses 6 and 11. This tendency corresponded to an intensification of the motif of sin. In verse 16 the cleansing of the holy place was originally related to the uncleanness brought about by the failures and sins of the Israelites. In verse 21 the motif of sin placed upon the goat was further emphasized by the addition of further concepts of sin [see 89, I.276]. Both of these directions of the priestly document's involvement in Leviticus 16 were grounded in a third tendency. Through an intensified consciousness of the holiness of Yahweh in relation to human sinfulness, there was also an increased separation of the cultic event from everyday reality. In verse 2, P emphasized that Aaron could not be in the most holy place at all times or he might die by viewing Yahweh's presence in the cloud. In verse 13 reference is made once again to this motif. In verse 17, P stressed the fact that no one could be present during Aaron's atoning activity in the holy place. In verse 19 the blood ritual of great atonement on the altar was expanded. In verse 24 emphasis was placed on the washing of the priest in the holy place. In this tendency one finally finds the introduction of an apodictic purification command in verses 26a and 28. The intensified consciousness of the sinfulness of man corresponds to the greater awareness of Yahweh's holiness. From that point, we can understand the emphasizing of the atonement for priest and people as well as the stress placed on the holiness of the cultic event. The addition to P in Leviticus 16:29-34a increased the goal of the ritual of the Day of Atonement to include the whole community. While atonement was achieved for all the people at the holy place, it was mediated through rest from work and fasts in the course of events. Finally, the Day of Atonement was placed on the tenth day of the seventh month, and the carrying out of the Aaronic high priesthood was commanded.

In that way we encounter the question concerning the history of transmission of the *prepriestly writing's ritualistic tradition*, which makes possible a look into the history of the Day of Atonement. The first indication is given in the introductory formula of the Azazel ritual in verse 20*b*: "He shall present . . . ." Verse 20*b* is tied to the preceding concluding formula in verse 20*a*: "And when he has made an end of atoning for the holy place." Thus, verse 20*ab* points to the fact that the ritual of Azazel's goat was originally independent of the act of atoning for the holy place [92.61]. Likewise it also points to the presentation of the goat as a sin offering for the cleansing of the holy place in verse 9, which is introduced by a formula that corresponds to verse 20*b*. The ritual of the Day of Atonement set forth by P is so formulated that a ritual reaching back into the preexilic time involving the atoning of the holy place was interpreted by the ritual of Azazel's goat, dating from the pre-Israelite period that brought about atonement for all the people of Israel. Those two rituals were so closely tied together that they were fused by a ritual of atonement. Thereby the ritual of the "atoning of the holy place" forms the framework for the ritual of Azazel's goat. [19] In this connection the ritual of the incense and cleansing of the priest was introduced. In this way the history of the transmission of Leviticus 16 is sketched as a mirror reflecting the cult development of the Day of Atonement.

2. The Experience of Reality in the Postexilic Day of Atonement

In the ritual of Azazel we are taken once again back into the earliest epoch of Israel's development, reaching back into the nomadic period. Thus the assumption that the Azazel ritual was originally the placating of a desert demon cannot be proven.[20] As in the apotropaic blood ritual of the nomadic passover, it is a matter of warding off demonic influences and powers that bring about destruction. In the process of bringing Yahweh into the ritual, it was reshaped to the point that it no longer involved a placating of Azazel but rather the driving forth of evil from Yahweh's area. Thus the ritual was increasingly interpreted in the context of the atonement theme.

The Azazel ritual in the form transmitted in Leviticus 16 allows conclusions to be drawn concerning the understanding of sin involved with it. Sins were understood as material objects that the high priest, standing before the people, can place upon the scapegoat. The animal took the sins of the people of Israel upon itself and carried them forth and suffered a representative death for Israel. In the presource writings, we find a ritual of the Day of Atonement that was further emphasized in the priestly writing. There the substitutionary atonement was not concentrated in the Azazel ritual but rather in the blood ritual originating in atoning for the holy place. The placing of the blood as the seat of life on the horns of the altar marked the death of the animal and the moment of the forgiveness of sin. "For the life of the flesh is in the blood; and I have given it for you upon the altar to make atonement for your souls; for it is the blood that makes atonement, by reason of the life" (Lev. 17:11).

If the animal takes the sins of Israel upon itself, then he suffers as a substitute the death that is the due of the evildoer in the deed-result relationship.

In the atonement process the people, as represented by the priest, were not the logical subjects of the activity, but rather emphasis is placed only on Yahweh who effects the atonement [63.217 ff]. Yahweh does not receive human righteousness brought about by works, but rather Israel receives of reconciliation by being freed from the relationship of fault and destruction. Atonement is not an event of punishment but of salvation.

The further development of this postexilic cult over against the preexilic period is evident. In the Fall Festival of preexilic Jerusalem one could participate in the festival event only if he had been found to be righteous or faithful to the community as set forth in the liturgy of "opening the gates." If the possibility is now transferred to the preexilic festival event of accomplishing loyal deeds to the community, such as community sacrifices [62.72 ff], then there was only a cultic justification of the righteous. The phenomenon of sin could not be cultically resolved but rather had only a significance, which excluded one from the cult and led into death. This significance was not directly transmitted by Yahweh but as a guarantee of the deed-result relationship was connected indirectly with the dimension of sin. An enrichment in the understanding of God is brought about when Yahweh renders atonement as being possible and creates reconciliation in the festival. Man becomes aware immediately of his denials and failures before God and is not left to the fate of his deeds, but rather is borne and held in fellowship by God. The major theme has become that man in his weakness and limitation has a relationship to God.

To be sure, the priestly document knows of clear limits of cultic atonement that are expressed in the phrase, "This person will be rooted out of his people" (Exod. 30:33, 38). In the event of grievous cultic failures, such as neglect of circumcision, nonobservance of the sabbath and the Passover, as well as purposeful breaking of the law "with a high hand," there was no atonement. Forgiveness as justification of the godless was still not conceivable in the postexilic period.

The discovery of God's readiness to forgive sin separates us from the religion of preexilic Israel and stands in contrast to the unforeseeable reduction of the universal claim present in the preexilic cult in Jerusalem. We have already seen that in the postexilic cult the contrast between man and God was explained anthropologically and was brought into center stage. From this point we can also see the separation of the political dimension of experience centered in the premonarchical festival events at Gilgal from that dimension of preserving the world from chaos rooted in the Fall Festival at Jerusalem. This latter dimension was originally mythical in nature with worldwide implications. With the reduction of the political experience one sees reflected the powerlessness experienced under the rule of Persia. From that point one can understand the decline of the universal-mythical demand of the preexilic temple that here the created world as nonchaos is constituted anew. If the determining force in the premonarchical Matzoth Festival event at Gilgal was a political-historical experience and the determining force at the Fall Festival in Jerusalem was the universal constitution of the world, then on center stage in the postexilic period would be the cultic event of the confrontation between God and man expressed in an anthropological dimension of the theme of sin. All three dimensions are basic for the human experience of reality in association with God. How could they be transmitted together in the festival event? Israel indeed discovered for itself three dimensions in the context of her relations with God, but was not able to bring them together to relate them to one another in a conclusive way in the framework of a festive resolution of reality. This represents the limitation of the Israelitic cult, which could only be transcended in the Christ event.

B.
FESTIVAL
AND JOY
IN THE
NEW TESTAMENT

Introductory Remarks

In the Christmas story we hear this famous statement: "Fear not! For behold, I proclaim to you a great joy, which all people will experience; to you is born a savior, who is Christ, the Lord" (Luke 2:10-11).

This cry of joy is a fitting title for the whole New Testament. This book is filled with the overwhelming experience of primitive Christianity that in Jesus Christ salvation has appeared in the world. This feeling is manifest throughout its writings—even the latest ones. Something absolutely new has its beginning there: the kingdom of God.

The apostle Paul said it no differently when he called Christ "the end of the law" (Rom. 10:4). That means, whoever belongs to the community of Christ has been freed from the law—he is no longer imprisoned; his life, his "service" completes itself now in a new dominion of the Spirit, no longer in the old written code (Rom. 7:6).

The experience of faith formulated in these verses speaks in a decisive way to the order of festivals in the Old Testament. They have lost their validity and meaning in Jesus Christ.

The Galatians were told by Paul that the keeping of the duties of the Old Testament, such as the Jewish festival calendar, would signify a return to idolatry.

> To be sure, at that time when you did not know God, you served idols which in reality were no gods at all. Now however, that you know God, or rather are known by God, how can you turn back again to the weak and beggarly "natural powers" and serve them as slaves once more? You observe *feast days*, months, and *festive seasons*, and years! I am afraid I have labored over you in vain! (Gal. 4:8-11)

Observance of the law and idolatry are set side by side—for Jewish understanding, an unheard of provocation. Rabbi Eleazar of Modiim (died about A.D. 135) appeared to have Paul in mind when he asserted: "Whoever desecrates the holy gifts, and *despises the festivals* and whoever breaks the covenant of our father, Abraham, that man deserves to be rejected by the world even if he has fulfilled many of the laws." [7, II. 754].

Insofar as Paul proclaimed the end of the law for the disciples of Jesus and under that call set forth his proclamation and work, the rabbinic verdict of "*despiser of the festivals* of Israel" was placed on the disciples and read back to Jesus himself. And in fact Jesus was very critical of the practice of piety in his day. He took for granted the late Jewish piety but at the same time broke from it "through his claims in these spheres" [54.206].

What details can be known concerning Jesus' proclamation in reference to festival and joy shall be presented in the following sections. Before we do that, let us make a few preliminary remarks concerning the criticism of the festivals in the Old Testament. This criticism served as a significant point of connection for Jesus and the early church.

VII. Prophetic Criticism of the Festivals

I hate, I reject your festivals. I cannot stand your assemblies. . . . Withhold from me the sound of your hymns! The playing of music I do not hear. (Amos 5:21, 23) No longer bring gifts, for your burnt offerings are nothing to me—they are an abomination! . . . Your festivals and your assemblies are very deeply hated by me . . . . (Isa. 1:13-14)

These are a few of the sharper statements of the prophetic criticism of the festivals. It would be wrong to understand these as a complete rejection of festival and cult. They were related to a specific situation and were directed to specific misunderstandings. Their intention becomes clear when one compares the blunt negative criticisms made in the name of Yahweh with the more positive demands: "Cease to do evil, learn to do good; ask about justice, relieve the oppressed; defend the right of the orphan, plead unto victory the case of the widow" (Isa. 1:16-17). Compare Amos 5:24; Micah 6:6; Hosea 6:6.

The prophets chastised the people for their lack of service in the Yahweh cult. The claim of the cultic celebration to convey and to make possible community loyalty was belied by the social realities. Wherever cult and everyday life were separated in this way, the festival became a blasphemy.

The prophetic criticism was directed against "the law unto itself" of religious ceremonies and holy sites and fought against the false security that was a part of that attitude. In his temple discourse Jeremiah described and cited that position. His description paralleled also the addresses of Isaiah and Amos:

> Do not rely upon deceptive works, saying, "Here is the temple of the Lord, the temple of the Lord, the temple of the Lord!" Rather improve your lives and your deeds in that you practice right with your neighbor and carry out no forceful acts against the stranger, orphan or widow. But now leave behind your deceitful words which are worthless. You are thieves, murderers, adulterers, and swear falsely, and offer to Baal, and chase after foreign gods, who do not know you. And then you come and enter before me in this house which is named after me and say, "We are delivered" and then do abominations again. (Jer. 7:4-6, 8-10)

The measure of this criticism was a totality of service to God, which surrounded the whole existence of man, of which Israel was well aware. The liturgies of the "gate" spoke to those pilgrims entering the sacred areas and called for a realization of service to Yahweh in everyday life [66.173-74]. Psalm 24 or Psalm 15 gives an example of this. "Lord, who may be a guest in your tent; who may stand on your holy mountain? He who is spotless and does rightly; who speaks truth from his heart and does not swear deceitfully; who does no evil to his friend and does not abuse his neighbor" (Ps. 15:1-3).

Whoever entered into the sacred area was confronted with a selection of Yahweh's commandments. At the same time a declaration of loyalty was required. The commands were not viewed as a "severe law"; their function was to establish a few fundamental negatives or "certain type of signs" on the periphery of life's circle. They also called for a responsible vigilance for Yahweh [89, I. 203 ff]. The prophets made themselves advocates and spokesmen for Yahweh; in his name they demanded community loyalty, for the destruction of the social life of the community was a sure index of disregard for Yahweh's will and broken fellowship with him (compare on page 79). Without basically disputing the legitimacy of a special cultic festivity, their criticism betrayed a concept of festival that found its full essence in the relationship to one's neighbor. In the proclamation of Jesus this thought was taken up and made more pointed; festivity and joy have their point of location in the relationship to one's neighbor.

VIII. "Profane" Festivity

1. Clean and Unclean

Concerning the question of Jesus' position in regard to the festivals of his time, the controversy story related in Mark 7:1-23, par. Matthew 15:1-20, concerning "clean and unclean" is a most interesting one. In the text one should observe an ongoing development; one concrete question receives many answers. The composition is divided into three scenes (verses 1 ff, 14 ff, 17 ff). The gentile Christian readers are given, in the parenthesis, important information for understanding the controversy (verses 2b, 3-4). Mark 7:1-23, as even all of the Synoptic tradition, demonstrates a developmental process. In the course of everyday usage of the Jesus tradition the voice of Jesus was linked to the thoroughly different voices of the shapers of that tradition.

The interests of the community were expressed freely in terms of interpretation and correction, in development and actual appropriation of the tradition. Exegesis, thus, always is confronted with the task of peeling back the tradition to the authentic kernel that Jesus used. In our pericope, verses 9-13 and 15 can be viewed for certain as authentic. These words of Jesus belong in a controversy situation; Mark 7:1-2, 5 gives a factual, possibly even the original, framework for the formulation [88.367 ff].

> Now the Pharisees gathered together to him, with some of the scribes who had come from Jerusalem. They had seen that some of his disciples ate their bread with unclean hands. And the Pharisees and the scribes asked him, "Why do your disciples not live according to the traditions of the elders, but eat their bread with unclean hands?"
>
> And he said to them, "You have a fine way of rejecting the commandment of God in order to keep your tradition: For Moses said, 'Honor your father and your mother,' and 'He who speaks evil of father and mother, let him surely die'; but you say, 'If a man tells his father or his mother, what you have gained from me is corban' (that which is due you from me is dedicated to the temple), then you no longer permit him to do anything for his father or mother, thus making void the word of God through your tradition which you hand on, and many such things you do." (Mark 7:1-2, 5, 9-13)
>
> And another time he called the crowd to him and said to them, "Hear me, all of you, and understand; there is nothing

outside a man which by going into him can defile him; but the things which come out of a man are what defiles him!" (Mark 7:14-15)

The opponents of Jesus were not concerned with hygiene. Handwashing before every meal was a part of the everyday ritualistic practice of cleansing, essential for the pious Jew. As the people of God, Israel was required to be holy and (priestly) pure; the danger of becoming unclean lurked everywhere in humans, animals, food, and other objects [7, IV 1, 353 ff]. Whoever "eats with unclean hands" violates the "tradition of the elders" and the fullness of the oral commandments passed on which reveal the law and casuistically give its intent. In the Pharisee's view the "tradition" was to be observed as much as the Law of Moses; the "fence" around the law and the law itself had the same dignity. In contrast, Jesus rejected the oral tradition—"to be sure radically" [52.201 ff]. In the example of the practice of corban, which, in reality, negated the fourth commandment, he revealed it as a means of circumventing the true will of God which seeks the salvation of man. He set the word of God (verse 13) against human tradition, which pretended to protect the divinity of God. Behind such criticism stood the conception that all worship of God is only meaningful "when God's being for man is never lost from view. Jesus lay bare the fact that in the understanding of his opponents, God is ultimately nondivine, for they negate the effect of his will imparted to man" [45.153].

Jesus attacked not only the tradition; he placed the Torah itself in question, as we see in the antitheses of the Sermon on the Mount and in Mark 10:1 ff. "Nothing outside a man which by going into him can defile him; but the things which come out of a man are what defile him." This statement is more than a radical pronouncement; it is an abolition of the law. Jesus did not dispute that a lethal destructive power brought about "uncleanness"—its location is in the heart of man. He did dispute, however, that there existed a magical, transferable uncleanness which could be present in objects. Ernst Käsemann has described very poignantly how all cult-oriented thought is conquered in this way. The "presuppositions of the entire essence of the cult, including its practice of sacrifice and atonement," were placed in balance. "The whole distinction between the *temenos*, 'the holy area,' and the profane," so basic to antiquity, was abolished. At once this word of Jesus destroyed "the foundation of ancient demonology." It demonstrated that Jesus certainly did not represent "a metaphysical dualism" or "the world view of antiquity with its antithesis of cultic and profane" [54.207-8]. In this way the question concerning the place of man before God was also set free from the area of the cultic. Clean and unclean must be viewed in one's relationship to neighbor. In a world which Jesus declared to be God's creation and thus fundamentally clean, purity is no longer to be achieved with the help of ritualistic practices.

2. Sabbath Healing

The Evangelists report on Jesus' stance over against the sabbath in many of the controversy stories. Historical inquiry is directed to the two Markan sabbath narratives (Mark 2:23-28; 3:1-6); other texts in reference to the subject are found in Luke 13:10-17; 14:1-6; and John 5:1-18; 9:1-41, and are to be seen as later additions and can be ignored here [71.79 ff]. According to Mark 3:4, Jesus met the lurking suspicion concerning his observance of the sabbath with the question, "Is it allowed on the sabbath to do good or to do evil? To save a person or to kill?" He gave the only possible answer by completely restoring a withered hand. This suggestive question allowed the hearer only an apparent choice; the alternative offered was not really one at all. It is obvious that "to do good" corresponded to the will of God; it was commanded even on the sabbath.

What room for movement does the law allow me? What can I do? These are questions that seem to be oriented to God as the Lord of the law. These are egocentrical questions. The shocking alternative of Jesus demands a change of perspective. The spotlight is now no longer directed on me and the area of what is allowed me but rather on others and what God demands for their good. That means loving acceptance that lies beyond all casuistry. The sabbath story concerning the sheep that fell into the pit points to this truth. "Who among you possessing a single sheep will not take hold of it and lift it out if it falls into a pit on the sabbath day? How much more is a man worth than a sheep?" (Matt. 12:11, par.). The example appealed to an experience that anyone might have had in showing spontaneous concern, one which demanded a reflection on the meaning of the sabbath. The command to love should determine the sabbath, as any other day, even if that means it loses its stature as a special day.

The purpose of the sabbath command and its later development was to assure just this special status. The sabbath was a sign and expression of election; its neglect, even in the least way, touched the very identity of Israel over against the nations. The sabbath command thus constituted "the very heart of the whole law." It weighed "as much as all the other commandments put together"; its obedience could bring special rewards. Indeed, if Israel would keep the sabbath two times, as prescribed, then her salvation would dawn. This evaluation explains why the Pharisees' "fence" of detailed ordinances, erected for the protection of the sabbath, was so high. It also explains why the death penalty was invoked against anyone breaking it [7, I. 610 ff; 72.6-15].

Jesus' words and his attitude gave support to the charge that he intentionally broke the sabbath. One should not be surprised that the Pharisees desired to put Jesus to death, in view of the sabbath controversy of Mark 3:6. It is quite likely historical. Death was the appropriate penalty for one who spoke so provocatively and at the same time so comprehensively of the sabbath. "The sabbath was made for man and not man for the sabbath" (Mark 2:27). "Thus, the Son of man is also Lord over the sabbath" (Mark 2:28).

The history of the reception of this statement in early Christianity illustrates its "shocking nature." Not only Jesus' opponents but even his disciples have handled badly the freedom that he declared. Matthew and Luke when they took over Mark 2:23-28 into their Gospels left out verse 27 with its criticism of the sabbath. Verse 28, which originally spoke about man in general (Mark's use strains logic), was viewed as a statement about Jesus as the Son of man corresponding then to Matthew 12:8 and Luke 6:5. The use of speech in verses 27 and 28 should be compared to that of Psalm 8:4: "What is *man* that you are aware of him and the *child of man* (son) that you accept him?" The post-Easter use of the title "Son of man" as a title of dignity for Jesus makes Matthew's and Luke's understanding possible. A characteristic limitation was thus placed on the words of Jesus. The sovereign limitless freedom which Jesus imputed to his community now, in contradiction to his intention, is reserved for him alone [54.207].

Rabbi Simon B. Menasha's (cir. A.D. 180] explanation of Exodus 31:14 is similar to that of Mark 2:27, "The sabbath has been given to you and not you to the sabbath." A distinctly similar thought is encountered in the Apocalypse of Baruch 14:18: "You say you want to make man the governor of your works in your world; thus it is recognized that he has been made not for the sake of the world but the world for his own sake" [7, II.5].

Neither quote had as its intent to criticize the sabbath [72.15; 13.81]. The following story of the pious Abba Tachna also does not contain criticism of the sabbath but tells of the conflict between the sabbath command and the command to love. The point of the story is that Abba Tachna, with the help of

God, succeeded in becoming righteous. His scrupulous questions, Has the sabbath been profaned? Where is my reward? showed, of course, only too clearly the power of a system that hindered love and could not be defeated.

> Abba Tachna, the pious, went to his city on the day of preparation for the sabbath. He had a pack on his shoulder. He met a leper who lay at the fork of the road. This one said to him, "Rabbi, show an act of mercy on me and take me to the city!" He said to himself, "If I lay aside my pack, how shall my household and I have what is necessary for the sabbath? And if I leave the leper lying there, I will have sinned against my soul." He took the leper to the city. Then he came and took his pack and arrived after the dark. However, everyone thought about what had happened and said, "Is this Abba Tachna, the pious?" In his heart, he also pondered, "I wonder if I have profaned the sabbath by carrying my pack into the city after dark?" In that hour God allowed the sun to beam . . . in that hour Tachna wondered in his heart whether he had received his reward? Then a voice was heard in heaven which said, "Go, eat your bread with joy and drink your wine with a cheerful heart, for God has found your work pleasing" [7, I. 391].

In view of a narrative such as this one, the radical nature of Jesus' criticism of the sabbath practice of his time becomes clear. The declaration that "the sabbath was made for man" (Mark 2:27) was just as wide-reaching as his statements concerning "clean and unclean" in Mark 7:15. Also here pious practice and religious activity are encountered in Mark.

To be sure, Jesus never abolished the sabbath; much more he recovered it as a time of possible blessedness. He freed man from every external compulsion and confronted him, on the sabbath as well as everyday, with the promise and demand of the love commandment. This call to a freer human responsibility was grounded in the full power of Jesus who announced and brought the rule of God. He foretold that God's interest even in the sabbath is in the salvation of man.

3. Temple and Synagogue

If one reflects upon Jesus' words concerning "clean and unclean" and also on his position on the sabbath, then it appears less probable that he "obediently participated in the festivals of his day" [91.227], "honored the cult and lived according to the church year of his people," and demanded "with great sharpness" a reverent attitude over against the temple and the altar, including the sacrifices [51.200-201]. The texts which support an opposing judgment can be used only with difficulty for establishing the historical Jesus.

1. It is certain that the polemical statement in Matthew 23:16-22, a woe against scribe and Pharisees, is secondary and is concerned with the formulation of vows and the casuistry of oaths. What stands there cannot be harmonized with Jesus' teaching against swearing and oaths and his unconditional truthfulness (Matthew 5:34a). In Matthew 23 the Jewish Christian church is speaking. That church participated in the cultic activity at Jerusalem and believed that it honored the temple and altar more than their Jewish opponents did. It criticized certain Pharisaic practices of swearing and believed that it more correctly swore by the temple, altar, and heaven.

2. In contrast Matthew 5:23-24 appears to present Jesus as obviously presuming the sacrificial rites. "When you bring your offering to the altar and there remember that you have something against your brother, then leave your gift there in front of the altar and go and be first reconciled to your brother and then come and bring your gift there!"

It is again the Jewish Christian church using these words to give legitimacy to its cultic practice. The original purpose of these words certainly was not such; they expressed much more an emphasis on the priority of forgiveness among humans, thus making the offering relative.

3. The so-called cleansing of the temple (Mark 11:15-19, par.) offers no help to us, for the reconstruction and interpretation of the narrative is uncertain. If one understands the course of events as a messianic renewing of the temple, then the critical element predominates [48.35-44].

4. Jesus' attitude to the temple might more quickly be discerned by looking at a similar critical passage (basically authentic) concerning *destroying* and *rebuilding* the temple. "We have heard him say, 'I will destroy this temple made with hands and after three days build another, which is not made with hands' " (Mark 14:58). Compare Mark 15:29, par.; Matt. 26:61; Acts 6:14. See also Mark 13:2, par.

This assertion shows that Jesus had no theological interest in the present temple, but in union with the Old Testament Jewish hope, expected a new one—even the eschatological temple. The erection of the new temple occurred in relation to his person, his appearance, and his proclamation.

The reports of the Gospels concerning Jesus' appearances at the festivals in Jerusalem (especially John's Gospel) do not refute this view. These reports did not wish to make evident "a conservative attitude of Jesus over against the Jewish festivals" but rather "his sharp opposition to the Jewish cult" [107.917].

Nevertheless, Jesus did not draw for his followers a demonstrable line of separation as had been done in the Qumran community. He was no "iconoclast." The official worship of Israel, which reached its highest expression in the great pilgrimage festivals, was made relative through eschatology or as Herbert Braun has said, made "of little interest" [13.84]. Consequently, it was not avoided or destroyed.

On the basis of Mark 7:15, which is a statement of victory over all cultic-oriented thought, it is difficult to conceive of any serious participation in the worship of the temple.

Paul Billerbeck has minutely reconstructed such worship in the day and time of Jesus.

At its center stood the completion of two sacrifices: 1. The presentation of the burnt offering in the holy place of the temple; and 2. The presentation of the Tamid sacrifice in which a yearling lamb was presented as a burnt or whole offering on the great altar of burnt offering which stood out in the open, east of the temple building. [8.2]

It is easier to conceive of Jesus' participation in the worship of the synagogue, for its services were completely noncultic. The form used there was similar to the later Christian worship services [111, *passim;* not in the beginning but at a later period, compare 4:19]. Relying here again on Paul Billerbeck, let us briefly describe synagogue worship [7, IV. 153-88; 9.143-61; 25.14-231].

A worship service in Jesus' day consisted of two parts. The first had a distinct liturgical bent while the second had a didactic character.

Part 1

(a) At the beginning stood the Shema within the framework of benedictions: "Hear, O Israel, Yahweh your God is one God! . . ." This great creed in which Israel confessed the oneness of God and his commandments was composed from sections of the Pentateuch: Deuteronomy 6:4-9; 11:13-21; Numbers 15:37-41. It was spoken by the assembled community. Every Israelite knew it by heart.

(b) Then followed the Shemoneh Esre (18), the eighteen prayers so called because it later consisted of eighteen benedictions (since A.D. 100). In Jesus' day only the first three and the last three of the eighteen existed [9.148]. The first benediction was worded: "You are to be praised, O Lord, God of Abraham, God of Isaac, and God of Jacob, Most high God, Creator of Heaven and Earth, Our Shield and the Shield of our Fathers! You are to be praised, O Lord, Shield of Abraham!" The last, according to a later number of the eighteen, read, "Place your peace upon your people Israel and bless us all the time; you are to be praised, O Lord, the One who creates peace!" The community responded from time to time with "Amen."

(c) Sandwiched in between the last two benedictions of the Shemoneh Esre was Numbers 6:24-26, or *Aaron's blessing,* "Yahweh bless you and watch over you; may Yahweh allow his face to shine upon you and be gracious to you. May Yahweh lift up his face on you and give you peace."

Part 2

This didactic section was devoted to the reading and interpretation of the scripture. Its elements were:

(a) The *reading of the Torah,* which was led by community members (three to seven, or more on feast days). The whole Old Testament was not read, but in a given period of time *(lectio continua)* the entire Pentateuch was read. In Palestine this was done in a three-year cycle and in Babylon in a one-year cycle. This reading was often interrupted by words of praise. A translator proclaimed the reading sentence by sentence into the western Aramaic language, for in the period before Jesus, Hebrew was no longer the mother language of the Jews in Palestine.

(b) The *reading from the Prophets* was also used, but in no established order of the pericope or in every worship service. For example, it was not used in the afternoon worship service of the sabbath or in the weekly worship services.

(c) *The sermon* was a free discourse interpreting the scripture and had become, since the second century A.D., a "domain of the scribes" [25.197]. At the time of Jesus, every member of the community could and did give the sermon. One presumed a state of self-qualification and preparation: "If one presents publicly the words of the Torah without pleasing the audience like milk and honey mixed together, then it would have been better not to present them at all. If one presents publicly the words of the Torah without pleasing the audience as a bride pleases her husband, then it would have been better not to present them at all"

[9.157-58]; Paul Billerbeck has cited some impressive examples of preaching; 9.158 ff; 7, IV. 174 ff].

(d) *The worship service* ended with the sermon [9.160-61] or with the *"holy" prayer* (since when?)—the Kaddish [51.192] which could have stood at another location—for example at the end of the reading of the Torah [25.94]. The Lord's Prayer of Jesus was related to the Kaddish. The oldest form available to us reads:

Glorified and sanctified be your great name in the
    world which
he has created according to his will.
Let your Kingdom come quickly during our lifetimes
    and our days
And the lifetime of the entire house of Israel.
Let your great name be praised forever and forever.
And respond with Amen!

The New Testament indications of the synagogue worship service in Luke 4:16-30; Acts 13:14 ff; and Acts 15:21 are very much like the ones found in the rabbinic sources.

According to the Gospels, Jesus often preached and taught and occasionally healed in the synagogue. Seen as a whole that is certainly historically correct. However, one should not surmise from that statement that Jesus had close ties to the synagogue. Such a connection is entirely unthinkable in view of his proclamation and attitude. The synagogue was the exemplary place of the Torah; the goal of every synagogue worship service was the sharpening of the law and its interpretation in "the tradition of the elders." Jesus radically rejected this interpretation and did not cease his criticism even of Moses. Thus, Jesus was not rejected from the synagogue without cause. One can only say this much: Occasionally Jesus chose the synagogue as the framework of his activity, but for the most part he chose to work outside that sphere. At this point in the chapter a provisional conclusion can be drawn: Any festival based on the words of Jesus must be set apart from the cultic sphere and be freed from ritual observances. The external framework of such a festival must be viewed as insignificant. The command to love must determine its many "profane" forms, for that command is at once the motivation and criterion of all festivity.

IX. Eschatological Joy

1. The Message of Joy

The Evangelist Mark prefaced his "Gospel of Jesus Christ" (Mark 1:1) with a statement in 1:14-15 that characterized in a comprehensive way Jesus and his proclamation: "And after John had been arrested, Jesus came to Galilee, and preached the gospel of God and said, 'The time is fulfilled, and the kingdom of God has drawn near; repent and believe the gospel!' " These sentences became the foundation for the terminology of early Christian missionaries. That fact is shown, for example, in the phrase (often used by Paul) "the Gospel of God" or the absolute use of the word gospel, in the expression "believe the gospel." It was Mark himself who spoke here and thus connected the voice of Jesus with the voice of the church. Around A.D. 70 he undertook, as far as we can tell, to be the first to relate the story of Jesus from his baptism by John to his resurrection. Mark wrote the first Gospel by reaching back into the rich Jesus tradition of the community. He collected words of Jesus, stories about Jesus, and brought into focus what was reported in the community about the passion of Jesus. He then carried out an interpretive redaction by arranging it in a unified historical-theological framework. Mark 1:1 and 1:14-15 are elements of this framework. In both places we confront the key word, gospel. The accent it receives is varied; on the one side, it characterizes the primitive Christian preaching of Jesus Christ (verse 1) and on the other, the proclamation of Jesus of

Nazareth (verse 14). Both represent the gospel. The choice of the same term makes it unmistakedly clear that Mark's concern is to ground factually and historically the primitive Christian gospel of Jesus in the Gospel of Jesus. For this reason Mark allowed the historical Jesus to deliberately and openly say, "Believe on the gospel" (verse 15). This demand did not belong just to the situation of Jesus at the beginning of his work in Galilee, but it reached even to the post-Easter hearers and readers of the word. The brief notice in Mark 1:14-15 introduces Jesus as one "who proclaims the gospel of God" as the herald of the "good news" of God. Therein we find a play of words on the statements of Deutero-Isaiah (Isa. 40–55) and at the same time a claim that the promise formulated there is now fulfilled.

The prophet that we call Deutero-Isaiah, which is Second Isaiah, because we do not know his name, quite likely was active in the Babylonian exile. He saw his task as comforting and lifting up the spirits of the exiles who were facing difficult questions of faith because of the length of their exile. "Comfort, comfort you, my people; says your God" (Isa. 40:1). In the name of Yahweh he proclaimed a new uncomparable salvation event— "in sublime words which up to that time had never been heard before but yet were very enticing" [89,II. 252]. Yahweh's coming is immediately at hand; he will reveal his glory to all peoples; "my salvation is near; my help emerges" (Isa. 51:5; 46:13). There will be a new exodus more miraculous than the earlier one from Egypt. It will be without "haste" (Exod. 12:11) under the personal direction of Yahweh. "But you will not go out in haste, and flee as fugitives; for the Lord will go before you and the God of Israel will join your journey" (Isa. 52:12). The exile will have an end; a new period of salvation shall appear; the exalting ones will return home to Zion. The prophet foresaw the procession of the liberated ones already miraculously marching through the desert:

Thus says the Lord, "I have heard you in a time of grace and
. . . will keep you and give you for a covenant of the people to
restore the land . . . to say to the prisoners, 'Go forth,' to
those who are in darkness, 'Come forth!' Along the roads
they will feed, and their pasture will be on all bare heights.
They will not hunger or thirst, neither will the scorching heat
or sun strike them down, for he who has compassion on them
will lead them to springs of water. And I will make all my
mountains level roads and my paths will be raised up." Shout
for joy, O heavens, rejoice, O earth! Break forth in joyful
shouting, O mountains! For the Lord has comforted his
people and will have compassion on his afflicted. (Isa.
49:8-11, 13)

For you shall go out with joy, and be led forth with peace: the
mountains and the hills shall break forth before you into
singing, and all the trees of the field shall clap their hands.
(Isa. 55:12)

The joyful messenger precedes the ones returning home. The
watchmen on the towers of Jerusalem see him "on the
mountains and break out in jubilation."

How lovely on the mountains are the feet of him who brings
good news, who announces a good message, who announces
salvation and says to Zion, "Your God has become King!
Listen, your watchmen lift up their voices, they shout
joyfully together, for they will see with their own eyes the
return home of Yahweh. Break forth, shout joyfully together,
you waste places of Jerusalem, for Yahweh has comforted his
People, he has redeemed Jerusalem. (Isa. 52:7-9)

In Deutero-Isaiah the "messenger of good news" is a peculiar
religious term for "characterizing the messenger of God, who
calls out the rule of God and introduces the eschatological time
with his productive word" [29.707]. The function of the
prophet himself is singled out in the term, "the messenger of
good news."

In chapter 61 of Isaiah, which stands under the influence of
Deutero-Isaiah (as does Isa. 60, 62, and the later text, Isa. 35),

the prophet is identified expressedly as the messenger of good news.

> The Spirit of the Lord God is upon me, because the Lord has anointed me *to bring good news* to the afflicted; to bind up the brokenhearted; to proclaim liberty to the captives and freedom to prisoners; to proclaim the favorable year of the Lord, and the day of vengeance of our God, to comfort all who mourn, to give them a garland instead of ashes, the act of joy instead of mourning clothing, praise instead of a spirit of fainting, that they will be called "trees of righteousness," planted by the Lord "that he may be glorified." (Isa. 61:1-3)

In the connection of this concept can be found the essential roots for the New Testament concept of "good news/gospel" [29, *passim*]. The Isaiah text that has just been quoted was taken up in the Jesus tradition; early Christian theology produced this connection in their terminology when they called Jesus "the one who proclaims the gospel" (Mark 1:14; Luke 8:1).

Deutero-Isaiah's enthusiastic promises remained unfulfilled. The return home from the exile took place without any accompanying miraculous events. The participants did not experience the beginning of "eternal joy over their heads" (Isa. 51:11). Compare Isaiah 59:9-11. The promise surpasses all earthly measure and predicts that nature will be drawn into the salvation event and "pain and sighing" will flee from the life of man (Isa. 35:10). This was not fulfilled, as well as the words concerning the blind, the deaf, the lame, and the dumb. "Then will the eyes of the blind be opened and the ears of the deaf opened. Then the lame will jump like a deer, and the tongues of the dumb will shout for joy" (Isa. 35:5-6). In Israel's conception the promises of Yahweh were not fulfilled in this statement but were always present—promises that have never been satisfactorily fulfilled. According to Gerhard von Rad, the Old Testament can "only be read as a book reflecting an enormous amount of expectation" [89, II. 331]. It shows us a people "who are always moving from new promises to a universal type of fulfillment of them" [89, II. 397]. Deutero-Isaiah's message of Yahweh's limitless love and his desire for the salvation of all men was the powerful pulse of this movement. The fulfillment of these promises had a universal dimension. The joy expressed in them became the essence of eschatological joy in general. The promise of the prophet remained as a living, unsatisfied and unfulfilled, promise. Within the Old Testament period these promises were often discussed (cf. Isa. 60–62 and Isa. 35) and then remembered in various ways in the Palestinian Judaism of the New Testament period. This remembrance included the concept of "messenger of joy" whom Rabbi Jose, the Galilean (cir. 110), considered to be the Messiah: "Great is the peace which the King, the Messiah, will bring when he reveals himself to Israel. He will begin his rule in peace: 'How beautiful are the feet of those who bring glad tidings, who proclaim peace . . .' " (Isa. 52:7) [29.127 ff; 7, III. 4 ff].

Early Christian tradition termed Jesus the messenger of joy and maintained that he had brought the long-awaited (since the days of Deutero-Isaiah) eschatological message of joy. (This message became the content of the Christian gospel.) Within it, the rule of God breaks in; the kingdom of God is already here.

Jesus himself characterized his work in a similar way. He saw it as a fulfillment or as a surpassing of the message of salvation of Deutero-Isaiah. Luke 4:16-30, depicting the appearance of Jesus in the synagogue of Nazareth, has the very same message. In the second part or didactic section of the synagogue worship, Jesus read from the Prophets (see page 107). He read from Isaiah 61:1-2a. In the Greek text of the Third Gospel, it is a free quotation that has been combined with Isaiah 58:6. "The Spirit of the Lord is upon me, because he has anointed me to *preach the gospel to the poor* . . . and to preach the acceptable year of the Lord" (Luke 4:18-19).

Jesus preaching on this text included the sentence: "Today

this scripture is fulfilled in your ears (*i.e.*, you are ear witnesses, verse 21). This Nazareth pericope is a text that has grown out of different elements [36.394 ff] and is greatly colored in its details by a pre-Lukan theology and placed in its present position by Luke as a means of setting forth the beginning of the activity of Jesus. In other words, we encounter here the voice of the church, not the original account of a tumultuous end of a synagogue service in Nazareth. The assertion that Jesus himself adopted the function of Deutero-Isaiah's messenger of joy rests upon good historical ground; it is confirmed by Jesus' eschatological cry of joy [51.107] that has been transmitted in the question of John the Baptist:

> Now when John had heard in prison the works of Christ, he sent two of his disciples. And said unto him: Are you he that shall come, or do we look for another? Jesus answered and said to them: Go and show John again those things which you do hear and see:
>
> "The blind receive their sight,
>   and the lame walk,
> Lepers are cleansed
>   and the deaf hear,
> The dead are raised up
>   and the poor have the gospel preached to them
> And blessed is he, whosoever shall not be offended in me."
> (Matt. 11:2-6; par. Luke 7:18-23)

Even if the background of this cry of joy reflects the formation of the church, determined by its interests in relegating and subjecting the Baptist to the role of forerunner of Christ (verse 2), there is still no convincing proof offered against the authenticity of Matthew 11:5-6, par. Luke 7:22 [15.135-36; 6.83-84]. This logion is a combination of free quotations from Isaiah 35:5 ff; 29:18-19; and 61:1-2. The lepers and the dead were not named in the Isaiah passage. "Their mention by Jesus points to the fact that his fulfillment of all the promises, hopes and expectations have surpassed all others" [51.107]. The listener would have noticed this extension of the fulfillment, which reached even beyond the limits of death. He would have been irritated, in view of the Old Testament context, that the call of Jesus reached its climax in "The message of joy will be proclaimed to the poor/ the message of joy will come to the poor." He would also be irritated by the weight given to the statement and its being linked to the word of blessing, "And blessed is the one who takes no offense in me." The other images of salvation in this list are caught up in the undertow of this latter one. That in fact is the reason for the controversy, irritation, and reproach.

The claim of Jesus and the uniqueness of his sending are explicitly set forth here. Jesus comes as the messenger of joy to the poor. One's reaction to this phenomenon brings about salvation or destruction. "Taking no offense in me" means that one will accept that the joyful message is for the poor and that the final salvation has dawned. The promise of Deutero-Isaiah has found its fulfillment in the work of Jesus and at the same time has experienced a challenging correction.

2. The Present of Salvation

Jesus has come as the messenger of joy. The central content of his message is the "rule of God" (= "kingdom of God/kingdom of heaven"). He could very naturally take up this vocabulary for it was well-known to his audience. That God would finally establish his rule once and for all was the hope and longing of the people. It was a hope somewhat different to that of the early phases of the history of faith of Israel, which had been expressed in terms of a definite change. The course of history would reach its goal and a new period would break in and a future beyond history would be revealed—without ups and downs—final salvation.

Jesus' statements concerning the rule of God can be reduced to one common denominator. Many of these appear simply to represent the later Jewish expectation while others break out of that frame. The problem is made worse by statements concerning the kingdom of God that appear side by side in future and present tenses. What did he say about the present and future? What did he hope for?

1. Jesus shared with the many pious of his day the concept that the "rule of God is in the future." Thus, he prayed in the Lord's Prayer, "Your kingdom come" (Matt. 6:10, par. Luke 11:2), as did the synagogue community in the Kaddish, "Let your kingly rule take place in our lifetime and our days and the lifetimes of the whole house of Israel in all quickness and speed" (see page 108). The impatient hope for the soon-to-be-realized kingdom "in all quickness" corresponds to the statement concerning its nearness in the statements of Jesus. "The kingdom of God is near." Jesus counted on a future visible rule of God and occasionally even set a date; even this generation will witness it. They will be witnesses of the beginning of the final rule of God, which will also be experienced by all men. "Truly I say to you, there are a few standing here who will not taste of death, until they see the kingdom of God coming in power" (Mark 9:1, compare Mark 13:30 and Matt. 10:23).

Although future, the rule of God appears close in the little parable of the budding fig tree: "When its branch has already become tender, and puts forth its leaves, you know that summer is near. So you in like manner, when you shall see these things come to pass know that it is nigh, even at the doors" (Mark 13:28-29).

The fig tree in contrast to the other trees of Palestine loses its leaves in the winter. In the springtime one can see the buds of new activity on its bare branches. It is a sign of the return of vegetation; summer is near. This picture in words tells us that the rule of God is very similar; it is near. The time remaining has been reduced to a minimum. The parable of the budding fig tree is a proof for the pressing imminent expectation of Jesus. This text and others (69.13 ff) leave no doubt that Jesus expected the coming of the rule of God to be near or in the immediate future as other statements seem to indicate. Along with John the Baptist and the Qumran community, he shared the pressing expectation of his time. This hope (conditioned by time) of a soon-coming of the kingdom of God "in power" (Mark 9:1) was not fulfilled. As an unfulfilled promise of God, it came to be a part of the treasure of faith of the Christian Church.

2. Jesus' message of joy was thus not discredited, for its unchangeable characteristic resided not in its futuristic declarations but in the statements concerning a *present tense* kingdom of God. Jesus maintained that the kingdom of God was present in what he said and did. This set him apart from his day and angered many of his contemporaries. In this way we encounter the unique nature of his self-understanding and gain a clear view of the self-conception of his mission. The first proof for this is the very authentic logion in Luke 11:20, par. Matthew 12:28: "But if I cast out demons by the finger of God then the kingdom of God has come upon you."

This word was "fulfilled in the eschatological feeling of strength which Jesus bore in his appearance" (according to Bultmann's formulation) [15.174]. It had its historical location in the controversy concerning Jesus' healings and demon exorcisms. That Jesus appeared as an exorcist is a presupposition, transmitted with accuracy and not doubted even by critical research. Deeds of wonder, especially exorcisms, were not unusual in Jesus' world. They, of course, had to be interpreted for some attributed them "to the power of Satan" (Luke 11:15). Such suspicion, which involved a very critical questioning of his authority, was encountered and answered by Jesus with the interpretation quoted above. His demon exorcisms came about "by the finger of God." What happens here is God's act. In reference to Exodus 8:15, Jesus made even a greater claim here. In his demon exorcisms, the kingdom of God had drawn near and was at hand. The bestowal of salvation on individuals with its deliverance of the body and the soul is qualified here as the rule of God. An event that just encompassed Israel or that transcended the world and history is not worthy of this name. Rather, this individual salvation is an expression of the rule of God—an indication and guarantee that God is acting and engaged in a struggle to carry out universal salvation [87.64-69]. In the background stands the conception that the rule of God must persevere against obstacles. Jesus' exorcisms were, for that reason, a declaration of the rule of God, because within them one sees that God's will for salvation has finally taken up the battle with the power of destruction. In pictures pregnant with meaning, Jesus brought to expression the end of this battle. In a visionary way the end of the struggle is taken for granted, as we find set forth in Luke 10:18: "I saw Satan as a burning star, fall out of heaven." Jesus saw himself as the stronger one who had already enchained the mighty one. "No one can break into the house of the strong man and rob his goods, if he does not first bind the strong man; and then he may rob his house" (Mark 3:27, par.).

A descriptive word is employed that makes use of all the power of suggestion to convince those listening of that point of view. In all that Jesus proclaimed and in his acts of healing, there is revealed the fact that a stronger man is now here; Satan has been defeated and has lost his power—that is a part of the rule of God.

A second proof for the presence of the rule of God and the battle that is involved is found in the equally difficult and exciting words of Jesus concerning taking the kingdom by force. "From the days of John the Baptist until now, the King of heaven suffers violence and the violent take it by force" (Matt. 11:12; compare Luke 16:16).

Here a turning of the age has taken place; Jesus looks back at a closed "Old Testament period of salvation." With John the

Baptist a new epoch has begun; the rule of God has broken in. However, God is still not "all in all; his rule is not universal or unresisted. The kingdom has broken in but only in the sense that it is met with resistance and those who oppose it try to prevent others from being a part of it" [54. 210 ff]. This is a strange conception that is quite different from what the current expectation desired and what it foresaw for the future. It is also quite different from what Deutero-Isaiah prophesied and the later Judaism hoped. The rule of God at this point does not appear to be triumphal. Men react with force to it. It is hindered in its effects.

How does that happen? Those doing violence are the opponents of Jesus. They are the pious who make salvation dependent on the minute fulfillment of the law, which brings about despair but not life. Jesus according to Matthew 23:13 spoke a woe against such people. The Gospel of Thomas compared them to the dog at the cattle pen.

Woe to you, you scribes and Pharisees, . . . you bar men from the kingdom of heaven; and you yourselves do not go in it; and those who would like to go in, you do not allow to go in. Woe to the Pharisees! For you are like a dog who sleeps at the gate of the cattle pen, which doesn't eat nor does it allow the cattle to eat. (Logion 10)

How can the rule of God be hindered? Ernst Käsemann has given an answer. "The rule of God can be hindered and snatched away because it appears in the simple form of the gospel" [54.211]. Jesus' message of joy must be accepted and believed, a fact which excludes its triumphal execution. Understood in this way, this logion of "taking the kingdom by force" must be seen over against Luke 11:20. Both passages speak of the already present kingdom of God. The one sees it from the point of view of confidence; the other from the point of view of opposition. In the exorcisms, the victory over Satan is experienced; his kingdom is robbed. When people resist Jesus, the kingdom of God experiences assault.

3. A third (more direct) proof for Jesus' assertion of the presence of the kingdom appears in Luke 17:20-21:

> And when he was asked of the Pharisees, when the kingdom of God should come, he answered them and said, "The kingdom of God comes not with observation; neither shall they say, 'Lo here!' or 'Lo there!' for, behold, the kingdom of God is in the midst of you."

Martin Luther's famous translation of verse 21 was worded, "For behold the kingdom of God is within you." As one of very many interpretations [69.26 ff] it has influenced the popular view in which the kingdom of God and innerness belong together. That was certainly not the original meaning. Jesus avoided the contemporary views, such as theories concerning "when the kingdom of God will come." Apocalyptic speculation and calculation and adherence to portents, which later characterized Christian apocalyptic (cf. Mark 13 and par.), were irrelavant to him (verse 20b). The concept that God's kingdom is at some time or at some place already present was irrelevant and unsuitable. One could not just run here or there and find it (verse 21a). No, the kingdom of God will not arrive according to a certain schedule; one does not have to seek it out, "for, behold, the kingdom of God is in the midst of you." That means that the kingdom of God is a reality experienced here and now in the works of Jesus. There where God reaches into a man's life through Jesus to effect salvation; there where men, such as Jesus, have enough courage and faith to understand such salvation as a gift of God—there the kingdom of God has already begun.

The kingdom of God is already here; that fact qualifies the time of Jesus as a time of fulfillment. All prior time had been a period of expectancy—an epoch qualitatively different from the present. For this reason there is a blessing pronounced on those who see and hear what now has happened.

> Blessed are the eyes which see (are able) the things which you see and ears which hear (are able) what you hear. For I tell you that many prophets and kings have desired to see those things which you see and have not seen them; and (desired) to hear those things which you hear, and have not heard them. (Luke 10:23-24; par. Matt. 13:16-17)

The unique character of this time as a time of salvation is underlined in the answer which Jesus gave to a reproachful question concerning why his disciples did not fast. And they come and say to him: "Why do the disciples of John and the disciples of the Pharisees fast, but your disciples do not fast?" And Jesus said unto them, "Can the children of the bridechamber fast while the bridegroom is with them?" (Mark 2:18b, 19a)

"The wedding feast has started; the bridegroom has been brought in; the sound of jubilation resounds out over the land; the guests are reclining at the festive meal—who could fast in the midst of all that?" [51.108]. This descriptive word makes use of a contemporary symbol, the time of marriage is a time of blessing. Formulated in a contrasting way, one would say that it is now impossible to fast and to mourn for it is the time of salvation, of festivity and joy.

From Mark 2:18 it is obvious that Jesus and his disciples did not fast in contrast to the Pharisees who observed two fast days each week (on Monday and Thursday) in addition to the required fast on the Day of Atonement. They fasted to do penance and to pray for the salvation of Israel. In contrast to Jesus and the Jews, the post-Easter church fasted on Wednesday and Friday [Did. 8:1]. They supported their new religious practice with a word of Jesus from Mark 2:20: "The days will come when the bridegroom will be taken away from you and then will you fast in that day." This is an excellent example of so-called church formulation.

If we look at the entire sayings of Jesus concerning the kingdom of God, then it is safe to say that Jesus reckoned with the *future* of God's rule and yet at the same time maintained its *presence*. He prayed, "Your kingdom come," and said also, "The kingdom of God is in the midst of you." In the history of gospel research there have been numerous attempts to solve this contradiction (obviously illogical) and to declare either the present or the future as the only authentic word concerning the kingdom of God. These attempts are doomed to failure. Historical criticism must recognize that the contradictory was characteristic of Jesus. How is that to be understood?

1) Jesus did not reduce the promise nor was he content with a partial fulfillment. He did not reduce the hope to an individual realm nor internalize it. The *futuristic* statements were viewed realistically and firmly—God is not yet "all in all." He took the promise at its word and seriously believed that the rule of God would involve the whole creation.

2) Whoever views God's rule as primarily future tense devalues the present tense. If salvation is viewed only as future salvation, then the present tense is devoid of salvation, a time of waiting, or perhaps a period of world damnation or a time of suppressed assurance of future salvation. The *present*-tense statements of the kingdom of God remove such a separation between present and future. Jesus demolished that barrier and set forth the present as the location of salvation; it is an integral part of "the period of salvation," "the full beginning of the whole future" insofar as it is disclosed in the proclamation of Jesus [6.82].

3) In the dialectic of future- and present-tense statements the creative power of limitless promise is attributed to the present. At last salvation and life are now achieved. The rule of God of which Jesus speaks is a dynamic greatness, which has *already* broken in but is *not yet* fulfilled and for this reason it

also stands endangered (Matt. 11:12). It is realized in the work of Jesus and in discipleship. An eschatology that is being realized, however, must speak both of the present and future tenses of the kingdom of God.

4) The most important aspect of the whole discussion is the presence already of the rule of God. It requires and is due all attention. John the Baptist (not a prophet of salvation) had proclaimed the dawning of the day of judgment. The God of judgment is now near at hand. Jesus appeared as a prophet of salvation. He was more than that for his clear assertion that "the new period of salvation had already begun" is without parallel [28.87]. He proclaimed that the God of goodness is now present. The time of God's love is here—an eschatological period of joy.

3. Blessed Are the Poor

Jesus was the messenger of joy. He proclaimed the presence of salvation. His cry of jubilation reached its climax in the statement, "The poor receive the good news and blessed is the one who takes no offense in me." God's goodness can now be experienced even by the poor. This truth was at the heart of Jesus' message and represented an intensification that obviously would be met with protest. For this reason it was followed by the statement, "Blessed is the one who does not take offense with me!" Blessed is the one who does not remonstrate against the fact that God's goodness is for the poor.

The way of Jesus shows how much his gospel aroused opposition. It brought him to the cross. The New Testament texts by which we know of his "gospel for the poor" allow us to recognize that even the Christian community at times hesitated to join in this joyful cry of Jesus. The "blessed is the one who takes no offense in me" was real for them and continues to be so.

A few observations concerning the Beatitudes will make that clear and will at the same time establish the identity of the poor.

The Beatitudes come to us in two versions: Matthew 5:3-12, par. and Luke 6:20-23. A contrast of the two produces many instructive comparisons. The tradition obviously shows signs of development as viewed in Matthew on the one hand and as seen in its different stage of growth in Luke. It also has a history of use within the church and has established a (theological) history. The considerable difference which exists between both versions provokes the historical inquiry concerning the original foundation of the traditions. Which Beatitudes can be traced back to Jesus? What were their original wording? What did they intend to say? To whom were the Beatitudes of Jesus addressed?

a) Matthew set forth as the prelude to the Sermon on the Mount (Matt. 5–7) a well-composed series of nine Beatitudes (Matt. 5:3-12).

I. Blessed are the "poor in spirit,"
 for theirs is the kingdom of heaven. (3)
 Blessed are those who mourn,
  for they will be comforted. (4)
 Blessed are the meek,
  for they will inherit the earth. (5)
 Blessed are those who hunger and thirst *after righteousness,*
  for they will be satisfied. (6)
II. Blessed are the merciful,
  for they will receive mercy. (7)
 Blessed are the pure in heart,
  for they will see God. (8)
 Blessed are the peacemakers,
  for they will be called sons of God. (9)
 Blessed are those who are persecuted *for righteousness sake,*
  for theirs is the kingdom of heaven. (10)
III. Blessed are you, when men shall revile you, and persecute you, and shall say all manner of evil against you falsely, for my sake. (11)
 Rejoice and be glad, for your reward is great in heaven; for so persecuted they the prophets before you. (12)

In this text one can see a conscious formulation at work. Eight of the Beatitudes, formulated in the third person, make up two strophes. The foundation for one and eight correspond to a type of circular composition. Actually the last Beatitude of Strophe I and Strophe II make use of the key word *righteousness* and in that way expound it [24.26 ff].

The ninth Beatitude is separated from the others because of its full detail. It is formulated as direct address (second person) and forms the bridge to the following words said to the disciples: "You are the salt of the earth. . . . You are the light of the world . . . so shall your light shine before men that they will see your good works and praise your father in heaven" (Matt. 5:13-16).

At the beginning stands the beatitude, "the poor in spirit." The enigmatic expression "poor in spirit" has been found in the Qumran scrolls [33.120 ff]. The pious ones who kept the law strictly called themselves the "poor." They viewed themselves as the "chosen ones," because they kept fully the law of God. Their poverty was not a material poverty; they were "poor in spirit." That concept stood parallel to (and almost synonymous with) a characteristically different self-designation, "the perfect in behavior":

> And he bestows upon them who have shaky knees a firm place to stand. To the defeated and naked he grants stability of the loins. And through those *who are poor in spirit* . . . he gives the hardened heart. And through those whose *behavior is perfect*, all the people of wantonness are destroyed. [1 QM 14.6-7]

"Poor in spirit" means humility, the opposite of haughtiness—a distinctive quality of the pious, an ethical quality, a religious attitude. The other Beatitudes in Matthew concern themselves with religious attitudes or a certain kind of conduct, or, in other words, with a humble mind (verse 5), with mercy (verse 7), with

purity of heart/truthfulness (verse 8), an active love of peace
(verse 9), and a desire or, as the case may be, the responsibility
for peace (verse 6 and 10; *cf.* also verses 11-12). Matthew lets
Jesus say further that the righteousness of the disciples must
exceed that of the Pharisees and scribes (5:20), righteousness
will be done (6:1), the disciples must actively seek it (6:33).
Only the blessing on those who mourn appears to have another
orientation. Mourning is not an attitude that one can receive,
but rather a situation in which one finds oneself. It may be then
that Matthew was thinking of penance, or those who were
doing penance, for their own sins and those of Israel. That
interpretation is not excluded [7, I. 195 ff] and in this
connection is worthy of consideration.

The evangelist Matthew placed in his Beatitudes certain
ethical qualities that are included in the promise made to the
blessed. At the beginning of the Sermon on the Mount, which
should be appropriately described as a primitive Christian
catechism, Matthew placed a "Christian tablet of ethical duties,"
which sets forth the "conditions for entrance" into the kingdom of
God [22.88]. It reminds us of the liturgy for entrance into the
Jerusalem cult [*cf.* page 18]. "Who may enter into the mountain
of the Lord? . . . He who has clean hands and a pure heart. He
who does not think deceitfully nor swear falsely. He will receive a
blessing from the Lord" (Ps. 24:3-5*a*).

That outlook is a part of the Jewish Christian milieu that
influenced the pre-Matthean tradition as well as Matthew's
theology. (Elsewhere in Matthew it is strongly evident.) Here
there is a marked new legalism: "Demands are made on the
Christian life" [22.87-88] and that is part of the problem. The
promise is reserved (again) for those who fulfill these demands.
The gospel for the poor threatens to become a gospel for the
perfect. Matthew 5:48 makes use of that very word and
formulates an enormous demand: "You shall be perfect, even as
your Father in heaven is perfect!" That intense statement has its
origins in Matthew's theology and not the joyful message of Jesus.

b) Luke sets forth only four Beatitudes, which seem much more primitive than those of Matthew (however, not just at first glance). Of course, these have also been redactionally colored. Their meaning has been decisively transformed by the fact that the Evangelist has added to them three corresponding woes (Luke 6:20-26).

Blessed are the poor, for to them belongs the
    kingdom of God. (20b)
Blessed are those who are hungry now, for they
    shall be satisfied. (21a)
Blessed are those who mourn now, for
    they shall laugh. (21b)
Blessed are you when men shall hate you and when
    they shall exclude you (and reproach you) and cast
    out your name as evil for the Son of man's sake. (22)
Rejoice in that day and leap for joy.
Behold your reward is great in heaven; for in like manner
    their fathers did unto the prophets. (23)
But: Woe unto you rich, for you have
    received your consolation. (24)
Woe unto you who laugh now, for you shall
    mourn and weep. (25)
Woe unto you, when all men shall speak well of you,
    for so did their fathers to the false prophets. (26)

The Lukan Beatitudes were completely formulated in the second person. Those addressed were the poor, the hungry, the mourners, the persecuted—people in crisis. Here it is not a matter of ethical qualities that one has or has not, but rather there is a concern for situations and feeling.

Luke thought of the poor obviously as poor materially. With the woe (redactional) against the rich, Luke attained a more detailed determination and establishment of his case. These woes agree with his typical tendency toward social criticism in one strand of his tradition. Wealth is in itself "base mammon" and whoever desires to be Jesus' disciple has to give up all he possesses (Luke 14:33). Compare also 12:13 ff; 16:9, 11, 19 ff, *passim*.

The Lukan Beatitudes are also encountered in Matthew in connection with the five others that we have already seen. He turned them into ethical precepts (poor in spirit, hunger after righteousness, and mourning), while Luke sharpened them in a reference to social criticism. Matthew and Luke possessed these as a common ground, and they can be traced back to a so-called "primitive discourse" that underlies both the Sermon on the Mount and Sermon on the Plain. This accounts for the amazing parallelism at individual points despite other differences. The four Beatitudes mentioned are therefore very old. Are they authentic?

The blessing of the persecuted certainly is not. It is too formal for the framework. Above all, it sets forth the situation of the early Jewish Christian church in which the members had to live under the threat of being banned from the synagogue. They would have been comforted by a prophetic declaration in the name of Jesus concerning their persecution by the Jews. This declaration encouraged them to find "joy through suffering" (see chapter 11).

c) In contrast, the three remaining Beatitudes are certainly authentic. Jesus bestowed salvation on the poor, the hungry, and those mourning.

> Blessed are you poor; to you belongs the rule of God.
> Blessed are you hungry; you shall be satisfied.
> Blessed are you who mourn; you will be comforted.

Poverty, hunger, and mourning are not "happy" situations. It is a paradox to call them blessed. Such a paradox does not fit well to be sure in the grammatical form of a general sentence (third person). In the proclamation of Jesus, it can only be understood as a direct encouragement in the second person [96.121 ff]. Jesus did not just speak about the poor but rather attended to them with a living word of blessing. This attention changed the situation; the fate of the poor experienced a turn for the better. The eschatological promised event has already begun; God's love comes to the poor in the encouragement with which Jesus comforted them and in the acceptance that he granted them.

Here it is quite clear again how greatly Matthew has shaped the Beatitudes. The change from second to third person is more than a formality; it is a linguistic device by which the encouragement of Jesus is transformed into a new demand. Encouragement is turned into admonition. The paradox is here set aside. This ideal picture of the pious names conditions that must be fulfilled if the blessing is to be valid.

Who are the poor?

Surely Jesus did not mean the *truly pious*, as Matthew said. A blessing on such people would have never led to conflict. Luke is closer to the historical situation when he describes the poor as those *socially deprived*. "Blessed are the poor" is with certainty addressed to them but not them alone. As in his answer to the Baptist, Jesus related his teaching to Isaiah 61:1-2. This Old Testament connection explains, along with other parallel concepts, who the poor are—those in despair, imprisoned, those with guilt and those mourning. The poor are the oppressed in an entirely comprehensive sense [51.115]. "They should not be limited to any single group. Their need cannot be limited to any particular type of poverty, hunger, or sorrow." The first Beatitude is intended for those "who have not made it"—those who have been deceived in reference to their rights and happiness, or those who are absolutely "in the darkness" [43.33].

The identity of the poor is also shown by Jesus' conduct. The circle of his followers furnishes concrete proof concerning those referred to in "blessed are you, poor." In a judgmental and reproachful spirit, Jesus' opponents asserted that Jesus associated with sinners, tax collectors, and prostitutes (Mark

2:16-17 par.; Matt. 21:31-32). They called him, therefore, the "friend of tax collectors and sinners" (Matt. 11:19, par.). Such association in their eyes disqualified him. A pious man, or a righteous man, or even a prophet (Luke 7:39) could not possibly associate with people who showed notorious disdain for the law. Certain dishonorable professions, above all tax collectors, were considered to be violators of the law, par excellence. They were, according to the rabbinical view, especially unclean and to be considered as the Gentiles. Anyhow, as collaborators with the Roman occupation, they were hated, and anything they did brought suspicion of requiring more than what was required and of suppressing and deceiving the people. The pious mentioned them in the same breath with robbers, deceivers, and adulterers (Luke 18:11).

From an external legalistic view, Jesus' followers appeared to be "tax collectors and sinners," just as despised as "the small" and the "insignificant" (Matt. 25:40, 45; 11:25, par.), *i.e.*, as people "lacking in every religious concept." For that reason they were damned to lead an unpious life. Jesus, himself, called them lovingly "the poor, the hard workers, and those who bear heavy burdens" (Matt. 11:28). He did not slander those who had been slandered, but rather promised and assured them of sharing in salvation, which most people viewed as being unattainable for them [51.114-15].

For Jesus these sinners were "the poor." Understood in this way, the first Beatitude is an expression of a new "theology." According to this divine teaching, God loves the lost and despised, the small and the simple, the beggar and those "who have not made it"—even these. He does not love "those who are full of assurance as the righteous and who despise all others" (Luke 18:9). Corresponding to this, Jesus said of his mission, "I have not come to call the righteous but rather sinners" (Mark 2:17). He shocked the pious with the statement that "tax collectors and prostitutes will enter into the kingdom of God—but not you" (Matt. 21:31; *cf*. 27, *passim*).

The parable of the Pharisee and the tax collector is to be read as an illustration of the first beatitude:

> Two men went up to the temple in order to pray; the one a Pharisee and the other a tax collector. The Pharisee stood and prayed thus with himself, "God, I thank thee that I am not as other men are, extortioners, unjust, adulterers, or even as this tax collector here. I fast twice in the week and give tithes of all that I possess." The tax collector standing far would not lift up so much as his eyes unto heaven, but smote upon his breast, saying, "God, be merciful to me a sinner." I tell you, this man went down to his house as one whose prayers had been heard by God, not the other man. (Luke 18:10-14a)

This example sets forth two men engaged in prayer next to one another. One is not able to think of any greater comparison— the absolutely pious over against the proverbial sinner. In this example two life-styles and the corresponding human attributes are contrasted. The *pious* man represents a strict principle of accomplishment. Without religious diligence there can be no reward. He sets forth his demonstrable accomplishments and knows that salvation is his privileged possession; he is chosen on the basis of his accomplishment and corresponding self-certainty; a deep chasm exists between him and other people (verse 11). The *sinner* hopes for inclusion without any prior requirements; he does not reckon on recompense but rather on love. He sees the kingdom with the certain knowledge that he cannot achieve salvation himself but that it must be received from the hand of God. That insight places him with the company of sinners.

Jesus in his comments clearly and definitively took sides: "I tell you, this man went down to his house as one whose prayers had been heard by God, not the other man" (verse 14). Compare 50.139 ff. This conclusion must have been an unheard of provocation for those Pharisees listening. For here is set forth a full reversal of values and relationships. Pious work

and moral conduct and the law, the very basis of religion, loses
its force as the criterion for righteousness. The parable of the
two men praying in the temple sets forth the antithesis between
accomplishment and grace, of law and gospel. Jesus maintained
that God was entirely on the side of grace. This message
divided the great minds of the day and still continues to do so.
Jesus wanted all people, even the pious, to receive God's
limitless goodness. Whoever receives that will gain a grandiose
change of perspective. Man's view no longer rests self-
assuredly on his own triumphant accomplishments. Also, he no
longer needs to be caught up in his own failures; he can direct
himself freely and quietly to the goodness of God; the blessing
on the poor invites one to all this and at the same time makes it
possible. It signifies the arrival of the love of God for the lost
and acceptance without prior condition and without reserva-
tion. That means absolute joy and happiness. "Blessed are you,
poor" encompasses in a pregnant way Jesus' message of joy. As
the message of God's joy in showing mercy, it is the basis of all
the joy of the poor. Now it can be said of the poor: "The poor
will rejoice in the Lord anew, and the poor among the people
will exalt over the holiness of Israel" (Isa. 29:19). He, God,
exults over you in joy, he renews you in his love. He shouts with
joy over you as in the exultation of the festive day (Zeph. 3:17).

4. The Joy of Repentance

The demand for conversion had been given to Israel by the
mouths of the prophets. Their words accompanied Israel's
history and were also very strong in the Judaism of the New
Testament period. The urgent appeal "do repentance" is the
product over and over again of a highly developed sensitivity
for sin. Every transgression of the law is indeed sin. Every
individual and general sorrow is understood as a consequence
of sin. The miserable situation of the people of God in

subjection to the Gentiles was a constant admonishment of their unforgiven debts. However, debts must be "worked off"—the sacrificial cult, the ritual of the Day of Atonement, sorrow, and even death could help to that end. Repentance was also achieved by every additional fulfillment of the law, including good works. "Whoever fulfilled a commandment won for himself a mediator, and whoever committed a transgression, an accuser. Repentance and good works were a shield before God's punishment" [7, I. 166]. Repentance is a bitter necessity and since one is confronted there with his own guilt before God, it is to be taken very earnestly. Its outer sign was much like that for mourning—sack cloth and ashes, prayer and fasting, tears and supplication.

The most earnest concern of the Essenes was to perform the piety of repentance. Whoever entered into the cloistered community of Qumran belonged from then on to the "converted ones of Israel" [Dam. 6:5, 8:16], to the ones "who do repentance for their transgressions" [1 QS 10:20]. "The band of Pharisees" should also be understood as a pronounced repentance movement. Along with the yoke of the law they took on themselves "the yoke of conversion." Their life was a constant state of repentance. The strict earnestness of their attitude of repentance can be concluded from numerous words and stories of the rabbinical tradition.

> Rabbi Eleazer in one word sharpened the need for sudden and permanent repentance. *"Repent one day before your death!"* In answer to an objection of one of his students that a man may not know the day on which he will die, *"For that reason he should even more repent today because he may die tomorrow. Thus, his whole life will be lived in repentance"* [7, I. 165]. "The gates of repentance stand constantly opened." Repentance means to quit evil works and make visible restitution for the committed wrong and start a different life. Thieves, robbers, and those practicing usury shall recompense the damages. Those lending money for interest shall tear up their bills of credit and loan no more

money even to a non-Israelite. Those who cast dice should break them to pieces and no longer play for money; "for tax collectors and those who levy duty, repentance is difficult" for it signifies not only giving up their profession but also the (impossible) restitution with 5% interest to all whom they deceived.

This repentance must be perfect. *"Only when one carries out perfect repentance which involves an uprooted heart will God forgive him."* There exists a strong warning against "a false repentance." *"Whoever is continually repenting will receive no forgiveness, for God will provide no opportunity for repentance."* In order to prevent a deceptive repentance the death penalty was placed over both the pious and godless "so that the godless will not want to pretend repentance when they see the eternal life of the pious and then say: 'The righteous stay alive only because they pile up good works and fulfilled commandments.' Thus their actions do not proceed from a pure intention." In this connection belong the famous words of Antigonus of Soko: *"You are not as slaves who serve a master in order to receive gifts, but rather you are slaves who unrewarded serve the master."* (Abot 1:3)

Even the most perfect repentance does not convey certainty of salvation. Even the righteous can be surprised by death while in a state of unforgiven sin and thus not have an opportunity to repent. For that reason it is said that "A living dog is better than a dead lion." It can also be said, "It is better to be a godless person who lives in the world than a righteous man who dies in his sin." Indeed, "when a man has been perfectly righteous his whole life and fails at the end, then he loses all."

Salvation cannot be forced. Naturally, the pious man must serve, start at the beginning, work daily under the "yoke of repentance" and hope that God's mercy will aid his own earnest endeavors. That means God spoke, "Open an entrance for me as big as the eye of a needle, and I will open to you an entrance into fortresses and castles." But beyond that there is a certain amount of deep uncertainty. The following story makes that disturbingly clear:

Once when Rabbi Jochanan B. Zaccai (died about A.D. 80) was sick, his students came to him in order to visit him. When he saw them, he began to cry. His students spoke to him, "Life of Israel, righteous pillar, strong hammer, why are you crying." He answered: "If one led me before a king of flesh and blood who is here today and in the grave tomorrow and if his anger was kindled against me, it would not be eternal anger. If he chained me up, his chains would not be eternal chains, and if he killed me, his killing would not be eternal killing. I could be reconciled to him by words and bribe him with money, and in spite of all that, I would cry. And now if one leads me before the King of Kings, the most holy one, may he be praised! He lives and exists in all eternity. In case his anger is kindled toward me, his anger is an eternal anger, and in case he places me in chains, they are eternal ones. If he kills me, his killing is an eternal one. In addition, I cannot be reconciled with words nor bribe him with money. There are two ways open before me; the one is to the heavenly Garden of Eden and the other to Gehenna. *I do not know which one I will be led to—is that not reason for crying?"* [7, I. 581]

The repentance of which the rabbinical text speaks is a genuine repentance—repentance in tears. Its motive is fear of judgment, and its characteristic sign is an external tension. Man takes upon himself the "yoke of repentance." He must serve and only then will God perhaps show him mercy. Salvation remains uncertain. The conversion demanded by John, the preacher of repentance, has a similar structure. His appearance in the wilderness, his clothing, his fasting, point to his mournful earnestness. The announcement of the approaching judgment brings God into focus and brings about fear and terror.

> Already the axe is at the root of the trees! Every tree which does not produce good fruit is chopped down and thrown into the fire. Whose fan is in his hand, and he will thoroughly purge his floor, and gather his wheat into the garner, but he will burn up the chaff with unquenchable fire. (Matt. 3:10, 12, par.)

Jesus also called men to repentance; he also spoke of judgment, but in a correction to the message of the Baptist, he pushed the motif of judgment to the periphery and placed at the center the invitation to share in salvation that is now available. The Baptist's God of judgment is surpassed by the present God of goodness [6.81]. In the small parable of the barren fig tree Jesus wanted to point out that kind of distinction.

> A certain man had a fig tree planted in his vineyard; and he came and sought fruit on it, but found none. Then he said unto the dresser of his vineyard: "Behold, these three years I come seeking fruit on this fig tree, and find none; cut it down. Why should it take up needed strength from the earth?" And he answered, "Lord, let it alone this year also, till I shall dig around it and put dung on it—perhaps then it will bear fruit." (Luke 13:6-9)

This parable incorporates motifs from the Baptist's preaching. It speaks of bearing fruit and plays on the picture of "an axe at the root of the trees" in order at once to correct that view: "Lord, let it alone this year also, till I shall dig around it and put dung on it. . . ." In other words, the present is released from the terrors of fear of judgment. In contrast to the Baptist, Jesus taught that one should understand this time as a time of God's turning to the poor and bestowing his salvation on them. In that way repentance is fully changed; it no longer stands as the characteristic sign of the last endeavor; fear is no longer its motif. To be sure, Jesus called for repentance, but at the same time it is clear that his imperative "repent" has lost its threatening nature. Such repentance is not effected in the same way as more serious repentance. It does not involve actively doing but rather allows the event to take place. Repentance is encountered as a free gift and can only be accepted. In place of the very serious "yoke of repentance" Jesus' invitation made use of the symbol of the "yoke" that at once shattered the paradox: "Come unto me, all you that labor and are heavy laden, and I will give you rest. *Take my yoke upon you,* and learn of me; for I am meek and lowly of heart, and you shall find

rest for your souls. *For my yoke is easy*, and *my burden is light"*
(Matt. 11:28-30).

The story of the tax collector Zacchaeus relates the story of
repentance that is a gift and not something attained:

> And he came to Jericho and passed through it. And, behold,
> there was a man named Zacchaeus, who was chief among the
> tax collectors, and he was rich. He took great trouble to see
> who Jesus was; and could not for the press, because he was
> small of stature. And he ran before and climbed up into a
> sycamore tree to see him; for he was to pass that way. And
> when Jesus came to the place, he looked up and saw him,
> "Zacchaeus, make haste, and come down; for today I must
> abide in your house." And he came down quickly and
> received him joyfully. And when they saw it, they all
> murmured and said, "He has gone to be the guest of a
> sinner!" Zacchaeus, however, stood before the Lord and
> said, ["Behold, Lord, the half of my goods I will give to the
> poor; and if I have taken anything from any man by false
> accusation, I will restore it to him fourfold."] But Jesus said
> to him, "Today salvation has come to this house for this one
> here is a son of Abraham! For the Son of man has come to
> seek and to save that which is lost." (Luke 19:1-10)

This narrative (quite likely late and a secondary addition based on
verse 8) is an outgrowth of the parable of the Pharisee and the tax
collector. It illustrates in an individual example that which Mark
2:13-17 sets forth more generally. Jesus turns to the tax collectors
and salvation comes to the sinners. According to Mark 2:17 Jesus
justified his conduct with an adage concerning the physician; it is
not without its irony: "They that are well have no need of a
physician but rather the sick. I have not come to call the righteous
(to the banquet of God's rule) but sinners!"

The final verse of the Zacchaeus narrative, "the Son of man
has come to seek and to save that which is lost," takes up these
thoughts and sets them in a theological framework similar to
I Timothy 1:15a: "The word is true and worthy of recognition

that Jesus has come into the world to save sinners." "To save sinners" is the major theme of the example of Zacchaeus and does not conform to the model of the "yoke of repentance." A man such as Zacchaeus would have no hope of that repentance, because it was practically impossible for tax collectors and those who levied customs to repent (see above).

Luke's contrasting model in chapter 19 contends that imperatives and demands do not help. If salvation depends on a lot of prior conditions, if it is legally conditioned, no one can be happy. In the name of God, Jesus desired that sinners receive salvation. For this reason he turned to the despised, excluded tax collector even before he could make restitution to those he had deceived. Originally, there was no indication of a restitution at all. All attention was focused on Jesus' turning to Zacchaeus without any apparent reason. Jesus took up quarters at his house, sought out his company, and honored him in the process. That means he accepted him without any prior conditions. What reproach and hatred could not do, goodness brought about. It effected freedom for repentance. Lovingly accepted, Zacchaeus could be someone else, free and assured. His repentance stands completely under the sign of joy. "With joy" he accepted Jesus (verse 6). In Jesus' example salvation and repentance have switched places. In Jewish thought repentance (an accomplishment of man) was the most serious of matters, "the presupposition that grants sinners the hope of grace." Now one can say "repentance is produced by grace" [10.76]. The gift of acceptance stands at the beginning. The experience of God's goodness that is achieved in it makes possible obedience (conversion). Repentance, which proceeds so directly from the experience of God's love, has no anxiety in reference to salvation. It is certain of salvation, and therefore its motif is not fear but joy. Its outer form is not a lament in "sack cloth and ashes" but the eschatological meal of joy.

In this festive meal Jesus is joined with those who have repented. Such table fellowship must have been very typical of his mission (Mark 2:15-17; Luke 15:1-2). For this reason his opponents made him to be contemptuous, "the friend of tax collectors and sinners, a glutton and a wine bibber" (Matt. 11:19, par.). The sharpness of that polemic is understandable when one considers "that in the Orient, the acceptance of a man at table fellowship is an honor even to this day; it means the granting of peace, trust, brotherhood and forgiveness, or in brief, table fellowship is the 'fellowship of life' before God—the most obvious message of the saving love of God" [51. 117]. The meal is a symbol of the messianic time of joy and as such a joyful festive banquet. Included in this, of course, are eating and drinking. "There is no joy (festivity) without eating and drinking" [7, II. 143]. Rich food and sweet drinks demonstrate that the trouble has been overcome and "that joy in the Lord is your strength" (Neh. 8:10).

The poor belong to this meal. Luke 14:12-14 indicates that friends, brothers, relatives, and well-off neighbors are not invited but the poor, the crippled, the lame, and the blind are. The parable of the great banquet sets forth under the perspective of "blessed is the one who is allowed to participate in the meal of the kingdom of God" the table fellowship of the poor. The thought that the poor belong to the festival is an old one; it points back to tradition. In cases of deuteronomic concern for the carrying out of measures of social correction such as is revealed in Deuteronomy 15, the concept had developed that future joy and *diakonos* belong together [91, *passim*].

Deuteronomy 16:11-12 is to be viewed over against the Feast of Weeks and 16:14 corresponds to the Feast of Tabernacles. "You shall be joyful before the Lord your God, you and your son, your daughter, your servant, your female servant, and the Levite who lives in your city, the stranger, the orphan, and the widow who is in your midst. Remember you were a servant in Egypt and observe and keep this commandment." In the report concerning the renewal of the

Passover by Hezekiah, II Chronicles 30:25-26, it is stated that
the whole community of Judah and Israel, including the
foreigners, rejoiced. According to Nehemiah 8:10, 12, the
festive community sent "fatty food" and "sweet drinks" to those
who had not prepared.

The Mishna (Pes., X. 16) proscribed for the poor at the
Passover feast "no fewer than four beakers of wine," even if it
must be taken from the "poor man's kitty." According to the
late text, Pesikta 100a, God speaks to Israel: "You have found
four members of the household: son, daughter, male, and
female servant. I also have four: Levite, foreigner, orphan, and
widow. I have said to you that you should rejoice with yours and
mine on the feast days which I have given you; if you do that,
then I will rejoice with yours and mine. These as well as those
will rejoice one day with me in the future . . ." [7, I. 853]. This
thought became a definite part of the Passover liturgy. In the
course of the meal the head of the house and the company at the
table lifted the Seder plates up and showed them at the same
time to the whole world and declared, "This is the bread of
sorrow that our fathers ate in Egypt." Immediately they added
the most unusual invitation in all the world, "Whoever is
hungry let him come and eat. Whoever is deprived, come and
share the Pesah; this year here . . . in the coming year in the
land of Israel. This year in slavery—in the coming year, free
[42.119-120].

To share in the meal is a gift. One is invited to the festival;
one cannot earn an entrance. For that reason table fellowship is
a symbol of a concern that is bestowed rather than something
earned by accomplishment. This bestowed concern stands at
the beginning of repentance—awakens it and bears it.
Therefore, in Jesus' example the joy of the feast is taken up and
carried further by the joy of repentance.

Repentance is the joy of man in the anticipated goodness of
God—and conversion is the joy of God in the finding of the lost
one; the parable of the lost sheep and the lost coin show that.

Then there drew near to him all the publicans and sinners to
hear him. And the Pharisees and scribes murmured, saying,
"This man received sinners and eats with them." And he
spoke this parable to them saying, "What man of you, having
a hundred sheep, if he loses one of them, does not leave the
ninety and nine in the wilderness and go after that which is
lost, until he find it? And when he has found it, with joy he
puts it on his shoulders. Rejoicing, he comes home and calls
his friends and neighbors and says to them, 'Rejoice with me,
I have found my lost sheep.' I say to you that likewise there
will be joy in heaven over one single sinner who
repents—more so than ninety-nine righteous who do not
need to repent. Or what woman having ten pieces of silver, if
she loses one piece does not light a candle and sweep the
house, and seek diligently until she finds it? And when she
finds it, she calls her friends and neighbors together and
says, 'Rejoice with me for I have found the piece of silver
which I had lost.' Therefore, I say to you, the angels of God
rejoice over one sinner who repents." (Luke 15:1-10)

Luke 15 is a "Gospel within the gospel"—the parables dealing
with lost things belong at the center of the proclamation of
Jesus. The Evangelist placed them within the context of the
controversies between Jesus and the righteous. The Lukan
framework in 15:1-2 is relevant but certainly not a historical
report; it is a summarizing theological statement. Subsequently, all sinners and tax collectors desired to hear Jesus. Just
as general in tone is the statement that scribes and Pharisees
were provoked by the conduct of Jesus and is one of the typical
intensified statements of the situation. The opponents were
upset about a theology whose major theme had to do with the
goodness of God. Above all, they took offense that this theology
was not just theoretical but was shockingly concrete and
practical in Jesus' mission.

    In this situation the parables concerning "lost things" offer
commentary on the actual practice of Jesus. These parables
maintain that God's love of sinners comes into play when the

hostility shown the godless is abolished. Jesus claimed to be acting in God's place when he accepted sinners. Understood in this way, the parables could be said to possess an implicit Christology. They report the Savior of sinners to be the Representative of God.

The parables of "lost things" want *to justify* the actual practice of Jesus. They all have the aim of trying to win over those who hold a different opinion. Parable discourse is the rhetorical means for achieving that purpose. The attention of the listener is turned to a word picture or a short-fixed scene that has as its goal the drawing of a conclusion in the neutral ground of the symbolical parable, which might then be applied to the discussion of the current problem. "Directing" the resisting listener to the proper judgment can be achieved much easier if the symbols used are quite clear. Jesus made use of parables from rural settings that were well known to every man. He introduced relationships and events that every listener knew and could evaluate. His parables referred to general truths, and this made them almost impossible to refute.

Even the double parable of the lost sheep and coin (piece of silver) relates that which is generally well known and accepted. The change in picture from the experience of a man to that of a woman underlines both the general application, as well as the formal structure, of the text. Both parables are formulated as one single question: "Who among you . . .?" In this way the argumentative, and at the same time, suggestive character of parable discourse comes especially into view. In the question the hearer is confronted directly with his own experience. He is so drawn and absorbed into the story being related that he is forced to give a reaction. Indeed, the question in the parable places pressure on him and requires an answer. However, there can be only one answer: Naturally, the shepherd who has found his sheep rejoices; any one of us would rejoice. It is obvious that a woman would be happy finding her lost silver coin after she had searched so long in her poor windowless hut. It represented her dowry and thus was very precious to her, because it was probably all that she had. All of us would rejoice under similar circumstances. To find that which has been lost is rightly joy, enthusiastic joy. And joy exists not only for itself but also for sharing and joyous participation. There is no doubt about that. Joy always seeks to experience itself in festivity, "Rejoice with me!" (Luke 15:6, 9). In the context of these readily accepted pictures of contagious joy in the discovery of lost things (Luke 15:7, 10) Jesus hoped that his critics would carry over the judgments made in the hypothetical realm to the factual. He set before them the only appropriate conclusion, "Thus will there be joy in heaven. . . . Thus will there be joy among the angels of God over one individual sinner who repents."

This formulation reflects the Jewish hesitancy of directly speaking the name of God and of keeping their distance from the activities and emotion of God. Therefore, God's name was circumscribed in several different ways, *i.e.*, with "The Almighty," "The All Merciful," "The Holy One—praise be to him," "The Father in heaven," or also "The Heaven" or as the case might be, "The Place." This last expression was used to replace the word heaven as a designation for God after it had acquired a "certain profane character" [7, II. 308-9]. "Joy in heaven" therefore means "the joy of God; God will rejoice." The same thought is expressed in "joy among the angels of God," that is, "joy in the company of God—God rejoices!" In Luke 15:10 where the topic is "joy in the presence of the angels of God," the name of God is a secondary accretion. Thereby, the description is placed a bit farther back into the tradition.

The parables concerning lost things are strong advertisements for the (theological) insight that repentance is God's joy. God rejoices at the repentance of a sinner in the same way as a shepherd does over the finding of a lost sheep. This comparison "reveals" Jesus' concept of repentance. There is no talk of accomplishments that must be carried out before God can act.

Repentance is put over against "being found" for God's highest joy is his joy in forgiveness—an anticipated forgiveness. Whoever comprehends and accepts that will no longer criticize Jesus' conduct in reference to tax collectors and sinners. Such is the practical consequence of God's "soteriological joy" [34, I.85 ff]. The parable of the lost son is also designed to change the critic's mind and win him over. This grandiose story also comments on and justifies the conduct of Jesus in that it proclaims God's joy in the return of the lost son.

A man had two sons. The younger of them said to his father, "Father, give me the part of your goods which belongs to me" (as an inheritance), and he divided his goods among them. Not long thereafter, the young son gathered all together and took his journey into a far country, and there wasted his inheritance in riotous living. And when he had spent all, there arose a mighty famine in that land and he began to be in want. And he went and joined himself to a citizen of that country; and he sent him into his fields to feed swine. And he would have liked to fill his empty stomach with the husks that the swine did eat; and no man gave unto him. And when he came to himself, he said, "How many hired laborers of my father's have bread enough and to spare, and I perish here from hunger. I will arise and go to my father and will say unto him, 'Father, I have sinned against heaven, and before thee, and am no more worthy to be called your son; make me as one of your hired servants.' " And he arose and came to his father; but when he was yet a great way off, his father saw him and had compassion and ran and fell on his neck and kissed him. And the son said unto him, "Father, I have sinned against heaven and in thy sight, and am no more worthy to be called your son." But that father said to his servants, "Bring forth the best robe, and put it on him; and put a ring on his hand and shoes on his feet; and bring hither the fatted calf and kill it and let us eat and have a joyful meal. *For my son here was dead and now lives again; he was lost and now is found.*" And they began to make merry.

Now his elder son was in the field, and as he came and drew nigh to the house, he heard music and dancing. And he called one of the servants, and asked what these things meant. And he said unto him, "Your brother is come; and your father has killed the fatted calf because he has received him safe and sound." And he was angry and would not go in; therefore came his father out and entreated him. And he answering said to his father, "Lo, these many years do I serve you, neither have I broken your commandment at any time, and yet you never gave me a kid, that I might make merry with my friends; but as soon as this, your son, was come, who has spent your living on harlots, you killed the fatted calf for him." And he said unto him, "Son, you are always with me and all that I have is yours. It is only fitting that we should make merry and be glad *for this your brother was dead and is alive again; and was lost and is found.*" (Luke 15:11-32)

The story of the lost son (or better the loving father) describes no typical course of action as set forth in the preceding parables of the sheep and silver coin but represents a special one. From the point of view of form criticism it is to be classified as a parable. In contrast to the simile that attempts to convince "by speaking only about undisputed things," the parable hopes to avoid opposition by relating the story in such a charming, warm, and fresh way that the listener cannot think of objections. In its distinctness it replaces the "advantage which the simile has in stressing the authority of that which is generally known and recognized" [52, I. 97]. One cannot deny the distinctness of Luke 15:11-32. Using all the art of folk storytelling along with its characteristic love for detail, such as the introduction of direct discourse and dialogue, repetition and refrain, he sets forth a suspenseful succession of dramatic scenes. The narrator attempts in this way to gain the attention of the listeners and to direct their thoughts and all their sympathy to a final argument for his case.

An excessive use of narrative skills is very important for the success of the story (which has been entrusted to us in a polished form), for it makes a demand on the first critical listeners who heard it told. In this regard part one describes in a

very plausible way the younger brother's premature arrangement for his inheritance. He then converts it into money and
sets out to travel—perhaps to one of the rich cities of the
Hellenistic Diaspora, where there were many opportunities to
live a life that the elder brother described as "living with
harlots."

To this extent the course of the action is not unusual. In the
rabbinic similes one meets many sons who "turn out badly."
One of the most famous of these goes back to the great teller of
parables, Rabbi Meir (around A.D. 150). "To what can this be
compared? There was once a king's son who fell into a wicked
life-style and set out on evil undertakings. The king sent the
boy's guardian after him and asked him to say, 'Come to your
senses, my son!' However the son said to him, 'How can I come
to my senses in front of you, while I am in this situation of which
I am so much ashamed?' The king sent word, 'My son, is there
any son who is ashamed to return home to his father? And if you
return, do you not return to your father?' " [7, II. 216].

Jesus' parable goes much further than that of Rabbi Meir.
While the prodigal son remains his father's son, he loses his
status as a Jew (that means, he loses his father) for he ends up in
the dire plight of tending swine. Such animals were the
epitome of uncleanness. If a Jew tended swine, the rabbinical
tradition regarded him as a Gentile and he was treated
accordingly [7, IV. 359]. In the view of Jesus' hearers, the
prodigal son in his dire plight was actually "dead," and every
conscientious Jewish father would have rejected him if he had
returned home as an unclean Gentile [87. 104]. He would have
reacted as the father did in the Apocalypse of Shadrach, which is
used as a commentary on God's reaction to Adam's sin.

> Tell me: what kind of father gives to his son his inheritance
> and then that son takes this and leaves his father standing?
> He goes from that place and becomes a foreigner and a
> foreigner's servant. When the father sees that he has been

left "holding the bag," his temper goes up in flames. The
father then goes and takes away from his son his inheritance
and chases him out of his dominion, for that son deserted his
own father.
What shall I do, I, the most exalted and jealous God? I gave
him everything; he took it and became a sinner and
adulterer. (Apocalypse of Shadrach 6:5-8)

This parable draws a conclusion in reference to God's behavior,
which is based on the typical behavior of man. If an earthly father
could carry out very bitter punishment, how much greater then
would God's punishment be, the strict judge! Measured against
that view, the father in the parable of Jesus acted in a very
unusual way. Without glossing it over, he establishes that the son
had "gone wrong," which is characterized in a charitable way as
"being dead" or lost. The manner and way in which the returning
son is received by the father was viewed by the audience of Jesus
as completely unexpected behavior in view of the story as it had
been told thus far. The father ran from the house to meet the son.
For an elderly Oriental that would have been most unusual and
also beneath his dignity to go in such a rush. He kissed the one
returning home as a sign of forgiveness, before the son even had a
chance to confess his sins. He did not make him become a servant
(verses 18-22), but greeted him as an honored guest, gave him
festive clothing to put on, placed a ring, the symbol of his restored
position, on his finger, and allowed shoes to be put on his feet as a
free man [50.130]. He prepared a great feast, "Let us eat and
make merry!" (verse 23). The joy of finding is painted in the
strongest possible tones in order to confront the audience with
the need of accepting the unusual behavior of the father.

The parables of Jesus are taken from life but do not just
portray life. It has been noticed over and over again that to a
great extent they contain *unusual features*. The conduct of the
father here is very similar to the highly unusual action of the
steward in the parable of the workers in the vineyard (Matt.

20:1 ff). It is just as unusual for *all* the invited guests to ignore their invitations and for the host then to allow anyone to come to his table (Luke 14:16 ff, par.). It is remarkable that *all* the maidens waiting for the bridegroom fell asleep and that those coming too late to the wedding feast are denied entrance (Matt. 25:1 ff). These and other unusual features have the purpose of increasing and centering the attention of someone who might be a stranger to the case. They help pinpoint the subject matter of the parable. Symbol and fact are here closely interwoven. At the same time the unusual features mark the spot where the judgment of the narrator and his audience might differ and, in the view of the narrator, might need to be brought together again.

Jesus attempted to captivate his audience with the picture of the overwhelming joy of the father in finding his son again. He hoped that they would give up their (pre)judgments and be able to accept his view concerning tax collectors and sinners. Subsequently, tax collectors and sinners, lost persons found again, were accepted by Jesus in the name of God without any requirements. They were loved of God, for repentance brings the greatest joy to God.

Jesus' evaluation was rejected by "the righteous." Their protest is pictured in the second part of the parable (Luke 15:25-32). This section of the parable gives additional information concerning the concrete situation of the discourse. The story of the loving father is directed to people like the elder brother in order to give them clarification and justification for the father's behavior and to win them over to his position. One plea is directed to them: "Make merry with us!" It sounds almost helpless when the father finally says, "It is only fitting that we should make merry; for this your brother was dead and is alive again, and was lost and is found." Thus speaks (helpless) love, which no one can compel but which invites and entices. Beyond the story itself, one sees Jesus campaigning for the limitless goodness of God. Every thought of accomplishment fades away before it. Since repentance brings joy to God, all people both sinners and righteous are called to the joy of repentance.

5. The "Fest" of Discipleship

Jesus' call demands an answer; sinners and the righteous must be found. The parables concerning lost things picture discipleship as an invitation and sharing in a fest and present following Jesus as primarily not a demand but a joy. In any case that is the point made by the double parable of the treasure in the field and the pearl:

> Again, the kingdom of heaven is like unto treasure hid in a field; it was found by a man and (quickly again) hidden, and for joy he goes and sells all that he has and buys that field (Matt. 13:44). Again, the kingdom of heaven is like unto a merchant man, seeking goodly pearls; who when he had found one pearl of great price, went and sold all that he had and bought it. (Matt. 13:45-46)

Both texts are also found in the apocryphal Gospel of Thomas; his (also in a secondary version) version of the parable of the pearl shows that originally the subject of the story was not a pearl merchant (as found in Matt. 13:45-46) but rather more generally, a common merchant. The Thomas-Logion 76 reads: "Jesus said, 'The kingdom of God is like unto a merchant with wares who found a pearl. That merchant was very clever. He sold all his wares and then bought the single pearl.' "

The hidden treasure and the very expensive pearl are favorite motifs of oriental storytelling [7, I. 674]; they give wings to fantasy and allow one to associate with happiness and well-being, wealth and blessing, an almost fairy-tale world. The men spoken of in the double parable go about their work in a very sober fashion. The poor day laborer (perhaps) in someone else's field, the merchant about his business—both were surprised by their magical discovery. (Matthew is the first to make the merchant into a pearl specialist whose discovery is the result of a long search.) A dream is fulfilled; the finder is filled with unsurpassing joy. The treasure and the pearl are worth so much more than all that the finders had previously possessed that it is easy to give up that which is less for that which is more. Surprise and joy are the theme of this pair of parables, and not (as often set forth) a readiness for unselfish sacrifice. "The kingdom of God does not come to man demanding the greatest kind of sacrifice . . . but rather it is the exceedingly joyful gift of God, who blesses men with his kindness and goodness" [34, I. 38]. Here it is not a question of decision, for "whoever is filled with joy by a treasure does not need to be pressed to make a decision. The decision has already been made. The treasure has already been plucked up by the finder" [53.143]. The activity of the finder is the obvious result of his experience; the joy over his discovery causes him to act. Discipleship is joy, because it is rooted in the happening of bestowed joy. Understood in this way, the double parable points to the characteristic arrangement of receiving and doing, of gift and task, or in theological jargon of the indicative and the imperative in following Jesus. In contrast to every moral code that confronts man as demand (imperative) there stands in the teaching of Jesus and in a corresponding way in Christian ethics, from the very beginning, a grandiose assurance (indicative). The essence of this assurance is that God has entered into his rule; he desires the salvation of his creation; and he now turns in love to all who are lost. Formulated and sharpened for the individual man, this call would be: you have been accepted and loved; all of this is for you; the offer of God's grace is for you; you do not have to accomplish anything to be saved; God has acted to bring you salvation. Human activity grows out of this (faith) experience; it is not a strenuous accomplishment; it is an obviously free act. The imperative says, act according to this experience; let the rule of God be visible in your conduct and felt by others; share in the salvation that you have experienced. Be merciful, for you (long ago) received mercy. This series of events is not reversible. For that reason Matthew is open to criticism for making the blessing of the Beatitudes, the (salvation) indicative, depend on the fulfillment of the imperative. The gospel becomes law when one says, "Be merciful—then you will receive mercy!" Compare Matthew 5:7; see page 124.

In the parable of the unmerciful servant (Matt. 18:23-35) there is a good example of both the interrelationship of indicative and imperative and the fact that one comes after the other. After a king had forgiven one of his servants a large debt, that servant went and threw a fellow servant into jail for not paying a debt, which in comparison was very small. His punishment was delivered with the statement, "Should you not also have had compassion on your fellow servant, even as I had pity on you?" (Matt. 18:33). The unmerciful servant refused discipleship; he did not give himself over to its joys and thus missed life. He could not, as Martin Luther once put it, "Do freely and joyfully that which pleases God." He would not be for his neighbor "a kind of Christ even as he had experienced Christ"; he lost his salvation because he was only concerned for himself and not his neighbors. Thus his story ended tragically [106.132 ff].

How the joy of discipleship can be expressed in an openness to one's neighbor can be found in the example set forth by the narrative of the *good Samaritan*. The setting of this parable was a conversation between Jesus and a scribe concerning the double commandment of love. In this conversation the scribe asked Jesus, *"Who is my neighbor?"* Jesus' answer was not in the form of a definition but rather a story:

A man went from Jerusalem down to Jericho. There he fell among robbers who stripped him of his clothing, and

wounded him, and departed leaving him half dead. And by
chance there came down this way a certain priest and when
he saw him, he passed by on the other side. And likewise a
Levite, when he came to the place, looked on him and passed
by on the other side. But a certain Samaritan, as he
journeyed, came where he was and when he saw him, he had
compassion on him. And went to him, and bound up his
wounds, pouring on oil and wine, and set him on his own
beast, and brought him to an inn, and took care of him. And
on the next day when he departed, he took out two denari,
and gave them to the host, and said unto him, "Take care of
him; and whatever you spend in addition, I will repay you."
*"Which of these three, do you think, was a neighbor to the
one who fell among the thieves?"* And he said, "He that
showed mercy on him." Then said Jesus unto him, "Go and
do likewise." (Luke 10:29-37)

To understand this story, one must know that in the first
century Jews and Gentiles stood over against one another in
irreconcilable hate. The Samaritans were excluded from the
Jerusalem cult. It was said of them that "they possessed no
commandments, not even a part of one," and they were placed
on almost equal footing with the Gentiles [50. 201 ff]. After
pointing to the lovelessness of the priest and Levite, Jesus
taught how to achieve love of enemy in the example of the
helping act of the Samaritan. He took care of the helpless man
without any regard for nationality or religious reservations; his
love knew no limits. Therefore, it corresponds to the love of
God that Jesus pointed to as the foundation of his command to
love one's enemy. "Love your enemy for God does also; he lets
it rain on both the just and the unjust" (Matt. 5:44-45, par.).

With this question, *"Who then is my neighbor?"* the scribe
wanted to know how the Old Testament command to love (Lev.
19:18) should be interpreted and limited according to Jesus'
opinion. Whom must he treat as neighbor and whom not? Who
is the object of my love? Behind that question stands the view
(just as obvious for today as yesterday) that the command sets

forth love as it were in a series of concentric circles. Thus there would be steps leading from relatives, to neighbors, to countrymen; foreigners and enemies would be beyond the limits of possibility. This parable requires a different kind of view. It begins with the one who fell among robbers and observes things through his eyes. A fundamental change of perspective is demanded from the hearer. Accordingly, the concluding question reads, *"Which of these three, do you think, was a neighbor to the one who fell among the thieves?"* Jesus was not concerned with the remote question concerning the object of love; that is certainly impossible to do. He was concerned with the subject (whether loving or unloving). Who treated the man as a neighbor? Whose neighbor am I? These questions so related make it clear that the command to love unconditionally applies to me and is not dependent on whether I find the other person deserving of love. I should be a neighbor even to my enemy. That is not demanded of me but rather it stands in the parable as an enticing possibility and an authentic life-style.

Jesus' ethic is primarily not one of demand but rather one set forth in narrative form. The uniqueness of his demand is obviously not in its content. Even his command to love one's enemy can be found both before and after him in non-Christian sources. Its uniqueness resides in the way it is related to his entire deeds and words and to the grammatical forms and structure in which it is expressed. Jesus entangled his audience in stories which illuminated and demonstrated what was demanded and at the same time opened the way for it to be carried out. Whoever listened was identified but also was led to identify with one of the roles of the story. He stood directly on the stage and was confronted with a role that would incite and free him for new conduct. The story gave him room to accomplish that.

An ethic in narrative form is in the position to preserve the sequence of indicative and imperative, as well as their interdependence, without becoming "legalistic." In the story of the good Samaritan, for example, a missed opportunity is always again set forth as a real opportunity. That is, no imperative and no unpleasant "Thou shalt," but encouragement and enticement. The parable sets forth possibilities and gives wings to them. It does not demand love but relates it as possible and hence makes it possible.

What finally happened on the road from Jerusalem to Jericho was a call from Jesus to the joy of discipleship—an answer to the incomprehensible goodness of God—a festival for achieving love of neighbor.

6. Quiet Certainty

The message of Jesus was colored through and through with the motif of joy. Very typical of his mission was the festive, joyful meal even though his way from the very beginning was accompanied by hostility and skepticism, doubt and failure (as the tradition clearly shows). How can these themes be woven together? Has not reality here been suppressed in favor of some fantastic hope? The answer to that question is clearly no. Jesus himself saw the discrepancy between his works (often modest) and the claim that the kingdom of God was present in them. The so-called parables of contrast show that he perceived the situation realistically and did not give up his hopes. In view of discouragement and doubt, he set forth pictures of encouragement in which the problematical present was linked together with the hoped-for future.

> To what shall we compare the kingdom of God or to what shall we liken it? It is like a grain of mustard seed, which, when it is sown in the earth, is less than all the seeds that be in the earth; but when it is sown, it grows up and becomes greater than all herbs and puts out branches so that the birds of the air may lodge under its shadow. (Mark 4:30-32, par.)

> The point of the story lies in the contrast between the proverbial small mustard seed and the two-to-three-meter

height of the great tree in the garden. The use of this picture in reference to the mission of Jesus says that even the most insignificant beginning or scantiness of result does not negate hope; the kingdom of God is certainly coming.

Matthew and Luke have placed the parable of the mustard seed with the one concerning the measure of dough. This combination is appropriate, for the latter parable has the very same purpose. "The kingdom of God is like unto leaven, which a woman took and hid in three measures of meal, till the whole was leavened" (Luke 13:20-21, par.).

A little leaven has the (wonderful) power of completely infiltrating a lot of dough; of little importance but yet offering a significant result; a modest beginning but yet a great conclusion. Over against all doubt, Jesus said, "The kingdom of God is like that."

The parable of the sower (Mark 4:3-8, par.) goes into much detail about present difficulties. The seed fell on the path and was walked upon, and on stony ground and could not grow, and among thorns where it was choked. And yet "others fell on good ground and grew up, matured, and brought forth fruit a hundredfold" (in the original rendition of Mark 4:8; compare 96.118 ff). Here attention was directed to the time of the harvest where in powerful contrast to the previous difficulties of sowing, one sees the ripened field and the blessing of harvest. "Even if failure after failure seem to appear, Jesus was still full of joy and certainty; God's hour has come and with it a rich harvest beyond that asked and beyond understanding. In spite of every failure and opposition, God allows hopeless beginnings to turn into the glorious end which he has promised" [50.150].

God brings about his kingdom; that is as certain as sowing and harvesting. The parables of growth seek to transmit that kind of certainty; they plead for quiet certainty and patience.

> The kingdom of God is like unto a man who cast seed onto the ground and then fell asleep and then awakened, night and

day. And the seed springs up and grows up—he knows not how. The earth *brings forth of itself* [automatically], first the blade, then the ear, after that the full corn in the ear. But when the fruit is brought forth, immediately he puts in the sickle, because the harvest is come. (Mark 4:26-29)

This picture contrasts the patience, indeed the inactivity, of the farmer with the automatic and incessant growth of the seed; the time of harvest comes of itself. The same is true of the kingdom of God—it also comes of itself, for it is the work of God and not man. The parable argues against every kind of activity directed to attaining salvation. In the time of Jesus the Zealots contended that Israel could help bring in God's kingdom by actively resisting the Roman occupation. Jesus rejected the Zealots' position and set his followers free (including himself) from the necessity of acquiring salvation by self-activity. He taught that his followers should look to the future full of trust and without tension. It is certain that the gospel will not lose its effect. Doubt is as absurd as saying that salt can lose its salty taste. This word concerning salt (colored by the tradition) originally had that meaning—or salt cannot lose its saltiness.

The rhetorical question, "Salt is good, but if the salt has lost its saltiness wherewith will you season it?" Mark 9:50a, par. is an impossibility as the following rabbinical anecdote shows. Rabbi Jehoschua B. Hananiah (*cir.* A.D. 90) was asked, "If the salt is insipid, what will one use for salt?" He answered, "The afterbirth of a mule!" Someone said to him, "Does a sterile mule have an afterbirth?" He answered, "Can salt then become insipid?" [7, I. 236]. Or is it unthinkable that God begins something and then leaves it half finished? That is incomprehensible. What God has begun he carries on to completion. This argument against doubt and hopelessness helps explain the parables of the tower builder and the king going to war (Luke 14:28-32) and also the parable of the assailant in the Gospel of Thomas. All three of these parables show the certainty of the kingdom, par excellence.

Jesus spoke, "The kingdom of the Father is like unto a man who wanted to kill a high official. He drew the sword from its sheath and struck it through the wall in order to see if his hand would be strong enough. Then he killed the high official." (Gospel of Thomas 97)

This shocking text encourages the listener to learn a lesson from the assassin, which is applicable to the kingdom of God. If an assassin does not carry out his task without first testing his hand to see if it is strong enough, then surely God would not have made a beginning for his rule if he had not been in the position to bring it into fulfillment.

These texts cited and many others point to the unshakable optimism of Jesus [34,I. 62 ff]. The nonsalvific present is neither colored over nor suppressed, but the present does not have the last word, for it stands there altogether in the light of God's future which is now beginning. The joy of which Jesus spoke and which he lived was not, therefore, some utopia in which reality was forgotten; it is eschatological joy, an expression of unlimited trust in God. In a unique way Jesus was very certain of the future. His faith in God gave him the power to have no doubts even in the face of the fallen state of the world. In spite of all experiences to the contrary, he campaigned in love for the salvation of the world, with courage, quietness, and certainty. His community, therefore, rightly called him "the beginning and end of faith" (Heb. 12:2).

X. Early Christian Worship

In primitive Christianity the joyful message of Jesus was taken over, but not simply repeated word for word. The Easter experience allowed Jesus to become the all-determining content of the gospel. Faith took hold of faith (and developed it over and over again theologically) and believed that the eschatological event of the cross proclaimed by Jesus did not tragically end but continued. Jesus' death and resurrection are the foundation and preservation of the definitive salvation of which Jesus spoke. The resurrection signifies God's affirmation of the Crucified One, of his proclamation and work. As an anticipation of the resurrection of the dead, it demonstrates that sin and death have been conquered and thus the eschaton has broken into history.

Such an experience of faith makes the believer into one who proclaims. The gospel of Jesus has been taken up into the gospel of Jesus Christ and is thereby preserved. Early Christian worship had the goal of passing on this joyful message and giving people the opportunity to share in the salvation of which it spoke.

1. Preaching

Proclamation of the gospel is the central life expression of the church of Jesus Christ. It is certain that Jesus sent out disciples "to announce the kingdom of God" (Luke 9:1-6, par.; 10:1 ff, par.). The so-called Great Commission includes the Easter experience in its outlook. After he has assumed his heavenly throne the Resurrected One continues to renew the mission.

> All power is given unto me in heaven and in earth. Go therefore and teach all nations, baptizing them in the name of the Father, and of the Son, and of the Holy Spirit; teaching them to observe all things whatsoever I have commanded you; and lo, I am with you always, even unto the end of the world. (Matt. 28:18-20)
> Compare Mark 16:15-16, 19-20.

The book of Acts relates how this commission was carried out. It describes the beginning of the Church in a complex, idealized

picture-making use of Greco-Roman historiography. It is easily
believable that the spread of Christianity was rather turbulent.
Acts 1:8 outlines a program in which the disciples under the
power of the Holy Spirit were called to be witnesses of the
gospel "in Jerusalem, in all of Judea and Samaria, even unto the
end of the earth." This picture is not exaggerated. The
missionary activity of Paul is proof of it.

What did Christian missionary preaching say to the
hearers? One of the first answers to that question must indicate
that it varied from place to place and according to the time and
situation. The Aramaic-speaking church had its own theological
profile and "taught" accordingly; the same would have been
true of the Hellenistic Jewish church or gentile Christianity.
These distinctions, however, were very rough in nature.
Within these realms of tradition, the accent was placed on
different subjects and various positions represented. In the
theological diversity of the New Testament this state of affairs
ended in fragmentation. Nevertheless, with all the diversity
there was a common foundation, the cross and Easter! (The
cross presupposes the proclamation and work of Jesus; Easter
signifies the presence of the ascended Lord in the power of the
Holy Spirit.) In spite of all the changing, controversial views of
the present, the cross and Easter remain the primary themes.
That truth is demonstrated, for example, in I Thessalonians
1:9-10, where Paul reminded the members of the newly
founded church of their conversion and summarized the
essential points of his missionary preaching: ". . . how you
turned to God from idols, to serve the living and true God; and
to wait for his Son from heaven, whom he raised from the dead,
even Jesus, which delivered us from the wrath to come."

That truth is also demonstrated in I Corinthians 15:1 ff
where Paul also called his preaching into remembrance—the
foundation of faith on which the Corinthians and their apostle
(and all apostles, verse 11) stood.

> Moreover, brethren, I declare unto you the gospel which I
> preached unto you, which also you received, and wherein you
> stand; by which you are saved, if you keep in memory what I
> preached unto you, unless you have believed in vain. For I
> delivered unto you first of all that which I also revealed, that
> Christ died for our sins according to the scriptures, and that he
> was buried, and that he rose again the third day according to
> the scriptures, and that he was seen of Cephas, then of the
> twelve. This [is the gospel that] we [all] preach; and to which
> you have come to believe! (I Cor. 15:1-5, 11)

This section of verses, I Corinthians 15:3b-5, is a quotation. The
(un-Pauline) use of words and the style of the meter and order
in the context all point to a handed-down tradition. Paul quoted
it precisely, making use of the pertinent jargon. He was simply
passing on what he had received. He stood, as far as this text
was concerned, in a chain of tradition and this tradition, which
he as well as the other apostles (verse 11) transmitted as *the*
Christian kerygma, was a very old one. It can be traced back to
the oldest Aramaic-speaking church in Jerusalem [49.95-96]. It
attested that salvation rested on Jesus' death and resurrection;
the reality of his death was underlined by the reference to his
burial. The reality of the resurrection was "proven" by the
appearance to Cephas and the twelve.

The events of Good Friday and Easter are not just simply
reported; they are interpreted and set forth as having salvation
as their end. In the New Testament there is no neutral protocol
for the events; the report is always connected with an
interpretation and application that stems from faith. We see
that in the phrases "according to the Scriptures" and "for our
sins." The statement that the fate of Jesus moved according "to
the Scriptures" is oriented to a *history* of *salvation* stance. The
other statement in which it is said that it took place "for our
sins" is interpreted in an ultimate *soteriological* sense. It
attempts to overcome the problem of the cross with a general
proof from the Old Testament. If read correctly, the scripture

demonstrated that the death and resurrection of Jesus is grounded in the will of God. It gives us a view of the salvation that we have won. Our sins have been atoned for vicariously and thus removed from the world. In his death Jesus became in a final and universal sense what he had been in life, the Savior and Redeemer of sinners.

The ultimate soteriological interpretation (dating before Paul) of the death of Jesus played a decisive role for the Christology of Paul. In contrast, it is very seldom set forth elsewhere in the New Testament. Compare in addition to I Corinthians 15:3; Galatians 1:4; Romans 4:25; 5:8; 8:32, II Corinthians 5:14-15; 5:21; Ephesians 5:2; especially Mark 10:45 and 14:25, par. As a theological statement, the kerygmatic formula was then, just as now, very inaccessible. It was not for that reason that early Christian preaching quoted it. On the contrary, it desired to make it evident in the stories of Jesus. That means that the phrase "he died for our sins" was concretely experienced in the fellowship of the church, especially in the Lord's Supper.

The missionary discourses of Acts (for example, Acts 2:14 ff; 3:12 ff; 4:8 ff; 5:29 ff, and elsewhere) are able to complete the picture drawn in I Thessalonians 1:9-10 and I Corinthians 15:3-5. In their present form they have been freely shaped by Luke, not just simply discovered. All the discourses give evidence of a common scheme that one might call a Lucan style or example of preaching, which with some variations incorporated a previous formula of the early Church. The main elements of these discourses were: (1) a point of connection is made to the situation, (2) christological kerygma, (3) scriptural proof, (4) a call to repentance with an offer of salvation. Paul's discourse in the synagogue at Antioch in Pisidia, recorded in Acts, is a good example of this style.

Paul spoke in the synagogue's worship service right after the reading from the Law and the Prophets; he related this situation to his own reason for preaching by giving an extensive history of salvation overview from the choosing of the patriarchs up to John the Baptist.

(1) Men of Israel and you who fear God, listen! The God of this people Israel chose our fathers and exalted the people when they dwelt as strangers in the land of Egypt. . . . Of this man's seed (David's) God, according to his promise, raised unto Israel a Savior, Jesus; when John had first preached before his coming the baptism of repentance to all the people of Israel. (Acts 13:16*b*-24)

(2) Men and brothers, children of the stock of Abraham and whosoever among you that fears God, to you is the word of this salvation sent. For they that dwell at Jerusalem and their rulers, because they knew him not, nor yet the voices of the prophets which are read every sabbath day, they have fulfilled them in condemning him. And though they found no cause of death in him, yet desired they Pilate that he should be slain. And when they had fulfilled all that was written of him, they took him down from the tree and laid him in a sepulchre. But God raised him from the dead. And he was seen many days of them which came up with him from Galilee to Jerusalem, who are his witnesses unto the people. (13:26-31)

(3) And we declare unto you glad tidings, how that the promise which was made unto the fathers God has fulfilled the same unto us their children, in that he has raised up Jesus again. As it is also written in the second psalm, "You are my son, this day have I begotten you." I have proved to you today that he raised him up from the dead, now no more to return to corruption, thus, he said, "I will give you the sure mercies of David." Thus he says also in another psalm, "You shall not suffer your Holy One to see corruption."(16:10)

(4) Be it known unto you, therefore, men and brethren, that through this man is preached unto you the forgiveness of sins; and by him all that believe are justified from all things, from which you could not be justified by the law of Moses. (13:38-39)

In the center of this preaching stands the kerygma of Jesus' death and resurrection. (In this connection, Acts stresses the contrast between the action of the Jews in crucifying Jesus and the action of God in bringing him back from the dead. Compare Acts 2:22-23; 3:13 ff; 4:10, and elsewhere.) As in the missionary discourses these speeches have been extensively developed and placed in a greater context. Thus, the early Christian preaching can be conceived in the way we have outlined or something similar.

The kerygma surely experienced other development as well. In fact, one might call the entire New Testament the "preaching" of early Christianity, especially the Letters of Paul. It was his desire that they be read aloud in the gatherings of the church (I Thess. 5:27; Col. 4:16) not just one time or only in the church that received it (*cf.* I Cor. 1:2). The letter is so fashioned that it could be read in the worship service or in part replace it (21.94).

The Jesus tradition must have also been an essential part of early Christian preaching. Form criticism has demonstrated that many of the stories of Jesus originally were used as examples in preaching, it was their setting. There they were used and in the course of being utilized, they were transformed and colored, up unto the time they were written down in the canonical Gospels, about the last third of the first century. Such stories gave to the kerygma a vividness that helped it be identified. They are a type of "religious propaganda" transmitted to advertise salvation. Their power to communicate is great, often greater for sure than discursive theological speech.

The story of blind Bartimaeus is an example of a bit of early Christian preaching (Mark 10:46-52 par.).

And as he (Jesus) went out of Jericho with his disciples and a great number of people, blind Bartimaeus, the son of Timaeus, sat by the highway begging. And when he heard that it was Jesus of Nazareth, he began to cry out and say, "Jesus, thou Son of David, have mercy on me." And many charged him that he should hold his peace; but he cried the more a great deal. "Thou Son of David, have mercy on me." And Jesus stood still and commanded him to be called. And they called the blind man, saying unto him, "Be of good cheer and stand up! He is calling you!" And he cast away his garment, rose, and came to Jesus. And Jesus answered and said unto him, "What do you wish that I should do for you?" The blind man said unto him, "Lord, that I might receive my sight." And Jesus said unto him, "Go; your faith has made you whole." And immediately he received his sight and followed Jesus in the way.

What purpose and what effect did such a story possess? It demonstrated salvific change. *The first scene* showed Jesus, the disciples, and the crowd (the many healed ones) on the way. Bartimaeus, the blind man, was sitting there alone. This represents a typical brutal tension between movement and stillness, health and sickness, and the crowd over against the lone man. *The second scene* brought the courage (of desperation) and hope into the picture; the desire for help must overcome massive hindrance. Many tried to keep the uncomfortable outsider silent, but he screamed louder. *The third scene* pointed to Jesus as the physician to the sick. Trust in him brings about "success." The blind man became well and whole; he could see again, he could walk, and was no more alone. "Your faith has made you whole." The tension is resolved; now is salvation. We must start with the fact that Christian preaching and storytelling made use of stories, such as these, for more than just pleasant remembering. There was no antiquarian interest in the tradition at that time. Preaching did not just recite what happened on one occasion in Jericho or elsewhere, but was interested only in repetition. The experience of Bartimaeus can be used here and now as a model of repetition; it becomes an actual possibility everywhere that the call to faith reaches its goal. In the church of Jesus Christ isolation is overcome, sins forgiven, sickness healed, salvation experienced and lived. This truth must be made concrete. One can see that in the circle of Jesus' disciples Zealots and tax collectors lived together and, thus, an example is set for the church, especially the Hellenistic one. They can see themselves in an homogenous community, well-integrated, because "in the Lord" all usual differences and discriminations are set aside. For those who have been baptized the following verse was true: "For as many of you as have been baptized into Christ have put on Christ. There is neither Jew nor Greek, there is neither bond nor free, there is neither male nor female; for you are all one in Christ Jesus" (Gal. 3:27-28). Compare I Corinthians 12:13; Romans 10:12.

In the ancient world in which Christianity developed this was no easy task either for the individual or the church. The conflicts in the church of Corinth show us how difficult it was to bring about that theological view. A story, such as about blind Bartimaeus, was one of many stories used in preaching to demonstrate and campaign for (outwardly) and encourage (inwardly) as well as remind the Christians what the church of Jesus is and how they should live.

2. Worship in Word

Early Christianity did not draw a strict line between the missionary situation and the preaching in the church. Among Jesus' disciples there could be no room for exclusive pious circles or cultic-ritualistic times and places (see chapter 8). The Christian worship service was basically an open one; it had to be. That does not exclude its own unique form (increasingly rigid, but better and freer). The fourteenth chapter of I Corinthians contains important information about the form of a worship service as it was celebrated in Corinth around the year A.D. 55 and very similar to others among the gentile

Christians. It was a matter of a worship service composed of word and prayer (4:19 ff).

The Lord's Supper is not mentioned in I Corinthians 14. Now I Corinthians 11 indicates that the Corinthian church knew of the celebration of the supper, but it did not belong, as can be seen, in every worship service. In view of I Corinthians 11:17 ff and I Corinthians 14, it is evident that there was no one worship service postulated for all of Christianity [37.61].

We do not find the exact course of the worship service in word outlined in I Corinthians 14. In the strife concerning speaking in tongues in Corinth, essential elements are set forth. They are: (1) different forms of proclaiming the word, (2) speaking in tongues and interpretation, (3) song and prayer. According to I Corinthians 14:6 the proclamation of the word took place in the form of "revelation, knowledge, prophecy, and teaching." First Corinthians 12:8 names in addition to the "word of knowledge" the "word of wisdom." There is no distinctive difference between them. The various forms of proclamation of the word were not sharply defined. They were always uttered in a rational way. This made them different from the ecstatic speech of glossolalia.

A *word of knowledge or wisdom* concerns itself with speech that reveals and informs concerning God's intent for salvation. First Corinthians 2:6 ff gives us an example (". . . it is God's secret wisdom of which we speak. It is hidden . . . but God has revealed it to us through his spirit. . . . ")

Revelation means the "declaration of concrete expressions of God's will for the present or future" [37.59]. Thus Paul went to Jerusalem because of a revelation (Gal. 2:2). In wrestling with the theological problem of Israel (Rom. 9–11) he achieved an insight into God's plan, a "secret of God" that should not be kept from the church in Rome (Rom. 11:25 ff).

Teaching has as its purpose to preserve and to pass on. To this belongs in addition to liturgical and catechetical traditions, the paraenetic material and the narrative source of the Gospels.

Many texts of the Synoptic tradition point to a setting in the teaching of instruction of catechumens. An interesting example of this is the parable of the sower [96.121 ff]. The office of teacher was already an important one in the time of Paul but also gained in significance in the postapostolic period.

Prophecy corresponds in its earliest function to that which we understand as preaching. Its task involved making real the message. Accordingly, the prophet relates the word to very definite questions of the present. He proclaims God's intention and the duty of man. He speaks to people "in order to build them up, exhort them, and comfort them" (I Cor. 14:3). According to the picture presented by Paul, the prophet is a *pneumatiker*, but not a visionary; his word is not characterized by ecstasy but by a clear consciousness and understanding. What he says is tested by others who possess the gift of "testing the spirits" (I Cor. 12:10). For Paul the gift of prophecy was in the highest rank of the "gifts of grace." But he never characterized himself as a prophet. However, according to I Corinthians 14:6 he spoke prophetically; his letters, as prophetic words, edified the church.

Ecstatic glossolalia in the Corinthian worship service obviously played a great role. That which is called in the Luther Bible "speaking in tongues" is speaking in nonunderstandable words and superhuman, heavenly speech that is seen as a gift of the Spirit. Seized by the Spirit and totally apart from oneself, enraptured, one becomes just a megaphone to scream, babble, or sing the glossolalia or irrational sounds.

Paul himself possessed the gift of ecstatic language. He did not debate that it was a work of the Spirit or that God was acting in it. However, he argued against overemphasizing the gift, for it involved noncommunication. In the church as it gathered, it should be practiced in moderation and interpreted so that all could participate. The essential purpose and decisive meaning of the worship service was, for Paul, the "edification" of the church and that occurred through prophetic discourse, whereas ecstatic rapture signified mainly self-edification.

> For he that speaks in a heavenly language speaks not unto men, but unto God; for no man understands him; he speaks mysteries in the spirit of God. . . . He that speaks in heavenly language edifies himself, but he that prophesies edifies the church . . . . Far greater is the one who prophesies than the one who can speak in heavenly language, except he interpret that the church may receive edification. . . . So also you, except you utter by the tongue words easy to understand, how shall it be known what is spoken? For you shall speak into the air. . . . Therefore, if I know not the meaning of the voice, I shall be unto him that speaks a barbarian, and he that speaks shall be a barbarian unto me. (I Cor. 14:2-11)

In his criticism Paul was thinking not only of church members but also of the guests present in the worship service, people who were showing interest in the Christian faith but had not taken the full step into the church. They ought to be reached and that could only be accomplished by prophecy that could be understood.

> If, therefore, the whole church has come together into one place, and all speak with tongues, and there come in those that are unlearned, or unbelievers, will they not say you are crazy? But if all prophesy, and there come in one that believes not, or one unlearned, he is convinced of all, he is judged by all. And thus the secrets of his heart are made manifest; and so falling down on his face he will worship God, and report that God is truly in you. (I Cor. 14:23-25)

Out of love of his brother and love to mankind in general, Paul gave up his rights to any self-expression of ecstatic speech: "I thank my God I speak with tongues more than all of you; yet in the church I had rather speak five words with understanding that by my voice I might teach others also, than ten thousand words in a heavenly language" (I Cor. 14:18-19).

In the strife over glossolalia, differing views of Christian worship and what it means to be a Christian confronted one another. Whereas Paul placed both of these clearly under the commandment of love, a part of the church obviously did not adhere to it. Their high evaluation of speaking in tongues demonstrated a theology which was not oriented to one's neighbor. The whole Corinthian correspondence gives testimony to that.

> This theology is colored by Gnosticism. In Corinth the gospel had been caught up in Gnostic thought and thus understood in a new way which brought about the protest of Paul. [94, passim]
>
> Gnosis (knowledge) was a religious movement of late antiquity, which was a religion of redemption much like Christianity but different because of its strong emphasis on dualism. Gnostic teaching stressed that the soul was the real self of man and was of heavenly origin; this view was the most important one. In the Gnostic myth various versions relate the fate of the soul. Its home was the heavenly world of light; it was originally a part or beam of a body of light, the so-called Urmensch. This primordial man fell into the power of demonic forces of darkness who tore him apart and with half of the particles of light in him, they created from chaos the present evil world of materialism. This soul, the real self of man, now lives as a stranger imprisoned in the body. Demiurge, the evil god of darkness, and his demons do all in their power to make the soul forget its origin. The highest divinity showed mercy on the fallen soul; he arranged for the redemption of the soul by sending his own son. As the demons watched, he came into the earth from the world of light, clothed in the tarnished form of man. He came as a revealer and reminded the particles of light of their heavenly home which they had forgotten. He woke the sleeping ones and gave to them knowledge of themselves, that is, their redemption. He also taught them how to return to the good world of light. When all the light particles have been awakened and redeemed, the evil world of materialism will sink back into chaos. [16.167 ff]

Certain Gnostic motifs (no fully developed Gnostic system) determined the theology and, thus, the conduct of the opponents of Paul in Corinth. We see that in the following:

They **demonstrated** their freedom over against the world of materialism by ascetic or libertine "disregard" for the body, *cf.* I Corinthians 5:1 ff (incest); 6:12 ff (prostitution) and 7:1 ff (marriage problems). They denied the resurrection of the body and allowed only a present resurrection in the spirit as is set forth in the Gnostic hymn in Ephesians 5:14: "Wake up you sleeper! Arise from the dead! And Christ will give you light!" (Compare I Corinthians 15.)

They **believed** that they had been chosen as perfect. The polemical rhetorical question of I Corinthians 4:8 plays on that theme: "Are you now full? Are you now rich? Have you reigned as kings without us?" The Gnostic had already seized salvation and perfection in the recognition that he himself was a piece of the divine pneumatic substance. From that recognition he saw himself as wise, strong, and glorious in contrast to being "fools for the sake of Christ," weak and being despised, factors that were true of Paul's life (I Cor. 4:10).

They **denied** Jesus, the historical man of flesh and blood and his cross and accepted only the pneumatic Christ. It was a Christology that allowed one in the spirit to say, "Jesus is accursed," a Gnostic Christian watchword that brought triumph over materialism. Paul opposed this with his own watchword, "Jesus is Lord!" (I Cor. 12:1-3; *cf.* 94:117 ff). Possessed of the consciousness of their pneumatic quality and strength, they despised the nonpneumatic people refusing to give in to them at all (I Cor. 10:23 ff) and proudly lived out their *gnosis*. They enjoyed their perfection by speaking in tongues in the worship service (I Cor. 14).

Such theology had turned the worship service at Corinth into a performance that broke up the fellowship and, thus, destroyed the Body of Christ rather than built it up. Divisions arose in the church (I Cor. 1:10; 11:18-19); each person sought his own interests and was not concerned with others (I Cor. 10:24). The strong had no solidarity with the weak, an assembly not for good but for bad (I Cor. 11:17).

Paul placed over against this chaotic fest, colored by Gnosticism, a fest of communication. Paul did not seek to please himself (only) but rather "to profit many others that they may be saved" (I Cor. 10:33; 14:17). All members of the church should do this. The command of love should determine their conduct, even in the fest. That means solidarity with the weak, under certain circumstances, giving up of one's freedom and showing compassion. These Pauline instructions for the worship service, so understood, are "nothing more than . . . an applied or practiced theology of the cross" [11.195]. Christian festivity in following Jesus will, therefore, never become ecstatic or triumphing over others. It looks in quiet certainty for the completion as it stands under the sign of faith, hope, and love. With the exhorting word "follow after love," Paul introduced his critical remarks concerning the practice of glossolalia in Corinth (I Cor. 14:1) and set before them the "song of love."

[I] If I speak with the tongues of men and of angels, and have not love, I am become as sounding brass, or a tinkling cymbal. And though I have the gift of prophecy, and understand all mysteries, and all knowledge; and though I have all faith, so that I could remove mountains, and have not love, I am nothing. And though I bestow all my goods to feed the poor, and though I give my body to be burned, and have not love, it profits me nothing.

[II] Love suffers long, and is kind; love envies not; love vaunts not itself, is not puffed up. Does not behave itself unseemly, seeks not her own, is not easily provoked, thinks no evil. Rejoices not in iniquity, but rejoices in the truth. Bears all things, believes all things, hopes all things, endures all things.

[III] Love never fails; but whether there be prophecies, they shall fail; whether there be tongues, they shall cease; whether there be knowledge it shall vanish away. For we know in part and we prophesy in part, but when that which is perfect is come, then that which is in part shall be done away. When I was a child, I spake as a child, I understood as a child, I thought as a child; but when I became a man, I put away childish things. For now we see through a glass, darkly, but then face to face; now I know in part, but then shall I know even as also I am known. And now abide faith, hope, love, these three, but the greatest of these is love. (I Cor. 13:1-13)

This "song of songs," also the hymns of Romans 8:31-39 or Romans 11:33-35, demonstrates "that Paul was as good a poet as Luther" [4.28]. Whether he created these texts for use in the worship service, we unfortunately cannot determine. In contrast, it is certain that in the assemblies hymns and prayers were used in addition to the surprisingly varied proclamation of the Word. First Corinthians 14:13 speaks of "eulogy and eucharist." In verse 26 it is mentioned that "everyone has a psalm." What is meant by that can be illustrated by texts in the New Testament. The hymns to Christ in Philippians 2:6 ff, II Peter 3:18 ff; and I Timothy 3:16 were all early Christian psalms (or songs). Mary's song of praise (Luke 1:47-55) can also be seen as a hymn of jubilation in the church to express thanks that the messianic hope had become a reality in Christ, which had been promised to the poor in the Old Testament Psalms [21.88]. These songs resounded in the choir or in individual singing (with the response of the church, *cf.* 4:27-28) and perhaps accompanied by music and body movements [21.83-84].

Eulogy (giving praise) and eucharist (giving thanks) are well-known to us from the introductions to the New Testament Letters, which appear to be patterned after the beginning of a early Christian worship service [21.55 ff]. After the greeting, "Grace be to you and peace from God our Father and the Lord Jesus Christ" (I Cor. 1:3), there followed here, as there, the giving of thanks. Philippians [1:3 ff] is a good example of a prayer of thanksgiving and II Corinthians 1:3 ff corresponds to a word of praise.

I *thank* my God upon every remembrance of you, always in every prayer of mine for you all making request with joy, for your fellowship in the gospel from the first day until now . . . that you may be sincere and without offense till the day of Christ; being filled with the fruits of righteousness, which are by Jesus Christ, unto the glory and praise of God. (Phil. 1:3-5, 10-11)

Blessed be God, even the Father of our Lord Jesus Christ, the Father of Mercies, and the God of all comfort, who comforts us in all our tribulation, that we may be able to comfort them which are in trouble, by the comfort wherewith we ourselves are comforted of God. For as the sufferings of Christ abound in us, so our consolation also abounds by Christ. But we had the sentence of death in ourselves, that we should not trust in ourselves, but "in God which raised the dead," who delivered us from so great a death, and does deliver. (II Cor. 1:3-5, 9-10*a*)

Both prayers were related very freely by Paul to his situation and formulated in a very personal way; in addition to these rather freely composed prayers, one also finds more formal texts, such as the Lord's Prayer [21:99-118].

The worship service that was mentioned in I Corinthians 14 cannot be fully described with the elements just named. Nevertheless, we may conclude that the fest of the church of Jesus Christ was characterized by openness, as well as variety and freedom (*cf.* page 97 ff). Because of this, one should not conclude that it was without structure. The church was comfortable with this and any other forms as long as love was evident (I Cor. 14:1).

3. Baptism and the Lord's Supper

Next to the proclamation, one finds the actual rites of the worship service; what is said in the sermon is made visible in baptism and the Lord's Supper and could be experienced in a special way.

Whoever inquires concerning the understanding and practice of the Lord's Supper and baptism in early Christianity discovers that he is confronted with a host of *religionsgeschichtlicher*, historical and theological problems [16.135 ff]. In this present book it is impossible to go into these in any detail. The following remarks are therefore limited to Paul. A selection of Paul's view on the subject will be presented in an endeavor to establish aspects of Christian festivity.

In his source Paul found baptism as a general Christian practice and interpreted it over against the tradition of the Hellenistic community [16.136 ff]. Thus baptism brought about: (1) a cleansing from sins, (2) a sealing with the name of Jesus Christ, (3) a bestowing of the Holy Spirit, and (4) the granting of a share in the death and resurrection of Jesus Christ. The baptismal event was the conclusion of a process that had its beginning in the answer of faith to the proclamation. Baptism was not a part of the faith experience; it followed. In baptism, one experienced what faith was all about.

Paul used this experience in order to interpret the gospel. His comments on baptism unfolded the kerygma and demonstrated impressively the real nature of Christian existence. Thus the Corinthians were reminded at the conclusion of an exhortation of what they had experienced in baptism and were called upon to make it the foundation for their existence:

> Know you not that the unrighteous shall not inherit the kingdom of God? Be not deceived; neither fornicators, nor idolators, nor adulterers, nor thieves shall inherit the kingdom of God. And such were some of you! *But you are washed, but you are sanctified, but you are justified* in the name of the Lord Jesus, and by the Spirit of our God. (I Cor. 6:9-11)

In an analogous way, I Corinthians 1:30 also speaks of baptism as Christ granting unto us *righteousness, sanctification,* and *redemption.* In II Corinthians 1:21-22 we find the picture of anointing and sealing in reference to the same subject. "It is God who has *established* us with you *in Christ, and has anointed us.* He has also *sealed us* (baptism) *and given* the earnest of the *Spirit* (future salvation) in our hearts."

This quoted text speaks of the baptismal event without any ifs or buts, in the indicative and in the passive; you are washed, you are sanctified, you are justified. In baptism, we meet not human ability but God's activity, "He has established us in Jesus Christ. . . . " Becoming a part of the eschatological community of salvation is not dependent on accomplishment; salvation is shared as a gift. Baptism makes visible, preserves, and repeats what is said in the kerygma and what is, structurally speaking, very appropriate for the proclamation and conduct of Jesus, the precedence of the indicative over every imperative (see pages 151-52).

Baptism's character as grace is also emphasized in the text, Romans 6:1-14, a central passage for a specific understanding of Paul's view. There it is quite clear that the cross and resurrection are the actual content of baptismal faith. In baptism, the course of Jesus is actualized; in his death and resurrection, his work of salvation is transferred to the one baptized and becomes active in him.

Know you not that as many of us as were baptized into Jesus Christ *were baptized* into his death? Therefore *we are buried with him* by baptism into death; that like as Christ was raised up from the dead by the glory of the Father, even so *we also should walk* in newness of life. For if *we have been planted* together in the likeness of his death, *we shall be also* in the likeness of his resurrection. . . . Now if *we be dead* with Christ, we believe that *we shall also live* with him. Knowing that Christ, being raised from the dead, dies no more, death has no more dominion over him. For in that he died, he died unto sin once; but in that he lives, he lives unto God. *Likewise reckon you also yourselves to be dead* indeed unto sin but alive unto God through Jesus Christ our Lord. *Let not* sin therefore reign in your mortal body, that you should obey in it the lusts thereof. *Neither yield* you your members as instruments of sin but rather *yield yourselves* unto God. . . . For sin shall not have dominion over you, for you are not under the law but under grace. (Rom. 6:3-14)

The statements of Paul go back and forth between present and future, and past and future, that which has already happened and that which has not. On the one side, "We have died with Christ," and on the other, "We believe that we will also live with him." Christian existence between that past and this present completes itself under the sign of the death of Christ that the baptized one had imitated in baptism. The present is qualified as the time of faith. Life with Christ is still to come; it is the content of hope, but in a paradoxical way, it is already here in faith. The barriers of the future seem torn asunder, and the present seems to be a valid part of the future. This is true especially when we read in verse 4 that Paul encouraged the Christians to walk in newness of life, or in verse 11, "Likewise reckon also yourselves to be dead indeed unto sin, but alive unto God through Jesus Christ our Lord."

The statements of Paul also move within this tension in an analogous way, between indicative and imperative. In faith the new being has already been grasped, but the believer still lives in this world. He "has died in his sins" in baptism (Rom. 6:2) and, thus, has been removed from their power but at the same time one hears the imperative, "Yield not your members unto sin . . . " (Rom. 6:13 ff). In another passage we find all who have been baptized in Christ "have put on Christ" (Gal. 3:27). Elsewhere we encounter the demand, "Put on Christ" (Rom. 13:14). Indicative and imperative stand next to each other, in fact within one another, but always in the sense that the indicative carries the imperative. Baptism has bestowed upon the believer new existence. Now we are able and may and should participate in it; "If we are living in the Spirit, then let us walk in the Spirit!" (Gal. 5:25). What this means is expressed in Galatians 5:22-23, "The fruit of the Spirit is love, joy, peace, long suffering, friendliness, goodness, faithfulness. . . . " Viewing the baptismal event and remembering the baptismal experience, as Romans 6 shows, gives valuable training in the faith existence of the Christian. His life is completed in the dialectic of a redemption that has already been bestowed and one that still remains to be given. The believer is borne along (indicative) and also placed under a demand (imperative); he does not need to accomplish his own salvation; it has already been attained for him. Thus, he is now completely free to be ready and open for his neighbor, "in faith which works by love" (Gal. 5:6).

Christian existence is missing wherever this dialectic is smoothed over in order to achieve some questionable unity. Whoever pays heed only to the imperative ends up in a "legalistic" morality; whoever fanatically covers over the indicative ignores time and history as the location of the Christian life. He becomes exclusively for himself and caught up in the enjoyment of his own salvation; he forgets his neighbor. The church at Corinth appeared to be in danger of this last threat because of the influence of Gnosticism. It ignored the imperative, and baptism became a magical medium that produced a salvation that could never be lost. Paul addressed this misunderstanding with an extensive typological argument drawn from scripture (I Cor. 10.1 ff). Christian discipleship can find no security in the cultic–sacramental means. Whoever thinks he is in possession of such must say, "Wherefore let him that thinks he stands take heed lest he fall" (I Cor. 10:12).

Baptism incorporates one into the church and initiates one into a new life-style; imperative and indicative can be viewed together. Christian worship in general and this observance in particular have as their function building up "the Body of Christ." It accomplishes this by making the word of preaching visible and perceivable, thus signifying that we have been laid hold of and are free to reach out to our neighbor. To ascertain and to place oneself in the service of love is the content and goal of Christian festivity.

According to Paul, the *Lord's Supper* also had the same purpose. It mediates anew the same experiences as set forth in the completion of the unique act of baptism. What I Corinthians 12:13a (compare Gal. 3:27-28) says about baptism is also entirely true of the eucharist according to the tenth chapter of I Corinthians.

> Through one and the same Spirit, *we have all been baptized into one body.* (I Cor. 12:13a)
> The cup of blessing which we bless, is it not the communion of the blood of Christ? The bread which we break, is it not the communion of the body of Christ? *For we being many are one bread and one body; for we are all partakers of that one bread.* (I Cor. 10:16-17)

Even as baptism, the Lord's Supper makes present the work of Christ. It does not exhaust its potential in remembering but also grants an actual sharing in that it allows one to experience *salvation as fellowship* (that is obvious for Paul) and obligates one to participate. It is the "Supper of the Lord" only when the salvation effected "for us" by Christ is made a communicative experience in the church. The words of institution are generally theological in tone. They become an ideology when actual practice belies them. Paul had reason especially to emphasize the thought of fellowship in his Corinthian Letter, because the celebration of the eucharist there was obviously very far from the norm of effecting salvation through fellowship. In the church there were both social and theological tensions that affected the worship service and especially the Lord's Supper (see chapter 10).

When you come together therefore into one place, it is not possible to eat the Lord's Supper. For in eating every one takes before others his own supper and one is hungry and another is drunken. What? Have you not houses to eat and to drink in? Or despise you the church of God and shame them that have not? What shall I say to you? Shall I praise you in this? I praise you not.

For I have received of the Lord that which also I delivered unto you, that the Lord Jesus the same night in which he was betrayed took bread. And when he had given thanks, he brake it, and said, "Take, eat; *this is my body* which is broken *for you;* this do in remembrance of me." After the same manner also he took the cup when he had supped, saying, *"This cup is the new testament in my blood;* this do you, as oft as you drink it, in remembrance of me." For as often as you eat this bread and drink this cup, you do show the Lord's death till he come.

Therefore whosoever shall eat this bread and drink this cup of the Lord unworthily shall be guilty of the body and blood of the Lord. Wherefore my brethren, when you come together to eat, tarry one for another. (I Cor. 11:20-27, 33)

The details of what was going on in the Corinthian church and what theological motives may have been behind it are greatly disputed among scholars [94.233 ff]. It appears certain that the Lord's Supper was celebrated at the conclusion or high point of a normal meal of the church. This meal was apparently enjoyed in groups or cliques "in which the rich enjoyed themselves and did not deem it necessary to wait on the poor people such as the slaves and workers who were not in the situation to be able to get to the evening church celebrations on time. So these meals became a horrible show window of the social division of the church" [11.199]. It is probable that the Corinthians based their argument on a massive sacramentalism (*cf.* I Cor. 10:1 ff), which contended that the poor and those who came in late would not miss out on the sacrament at the conclusion of the meal—the most important part anyway. Paul explained that the Lord's Supper under these circumstances was "impossible"

(I Cor. 11:20). He reminded them expressedly that the Lord's Supper concerned itself with the Lord's death and the unity of his body, that is the church, and that it did not involve magical cultic practices. Salvation transmits social communication.

Other important motifs of celebrating the Lord's Supper that had already developed in the primitive church did not play a significant role for Paul. One of these was the motif of jubilation (in this regard, see the thorough treatment in 23.76 ff) which is experienced within the eschatological view; cf. Mark 14:25, par.; I Corinthians 11:26: "till he come"; Acts 2:46-47a underlines distinctly the aspect of joy: ". . . They broke bread together in various homes, *they shared their meals with gladness and singleness of heart, praising God and having favor with all the people." The Lord's Supper looks back to the salvific death of Jesus; it points to the present where Jesus' work of salvation will be realized; it also looks out into the future and anticipates the coming meal of final salvation; for this reason it is a celebration in eschatological jubilation.*

Paul's criticism of the abuses at Corinth made use of the proclamation of Jesus in word and deed according to the post-Easter expression. Paul indicated that his Lord's Supper tradition was taken over from the sources and then passed on by him to others. Its origin must have been in the Passover supper of Jesus [49.9 ff; 7, IV. 1, 41-76]. Jesus made use of the table prayer at the beginning and end of the main Passover meal to infuse it with *heilsgeschichtliche* significance concerning his approaching death. The bread that the host broke became a symbol for the breaking of his body. That is indicated in the original wording, *"This—my body. . . . "* The wine that was poured three times in the course of the Passover meal became a symbol of his blood that "is poured out for many," which will bring about universal atonement. That truth is also expressed in the original words of the cup, *"This—my blood* (blood of the covenant?) poured out for many" [*i.e.*, all; 49.132].

Jesus himself saw his death in the sense of an atonement for all mankind as expressed in Isaiah 53. That which determined his life is also fulfilled in his death, service, and existence for sinners [86, *passim*]. Mark 10:45 expresses it in words analogous to those rendered over the cup, "I have not come to be served, but to serve, and to lay down my life as a ransom for many." His openness to the lost, the acceptance of the religious outcasts, was a *de facto* removal of their sinful status, forgiveness, and atonement. Jesus' mediation of salvation was not accomplished in the cultic or ritualistic but by symbolic social communication. In the Last Supper he proclaimed that there was universal significance to the table fellowship that he had begun with sinners and tax collectors. The Lord's Supper, as a festival of his church, stands under that kind of obligation. Only when it gives a place for the work of Jesus, said Paul, is it really the Lord's Supper.

4. Worship in the Everyday World

For the disciple of Jesus, Christian worship is a place for testing love. All of Paul's statements concerning preaching, baptism, and the Lord's Supper attest to that [12.118]. The whole life of the Christian stands under the command to love and that is especially true of his actions in worship and feasts. Paul made it very clear that the distinction between holy and profane no longer existed. Jesus removed it once and for all see chapters 8 and 9). Worship and fest no longer have a special kind of status; they are now a part of the whole reality of the Christian, and as long as the command to love determines them, they are services of worship to God. This truth is implied in the caption that Paul placed at the beginning to his paraenetic section of the Roman Letter. "I beseech you, therefore, brethren by the mercies of God, that you present your bodies a living sacrifice, holy, acceptable unto God, which is your reasonable service" (Rom. 12:1). Here in cultic terminology (and occasionally elsewhere, compare 37.52 ff) the essence of Christian life is described. The formulation shows "the paradox, the depth of change" and "the radicalness of the conversion" [55.201 ff]. The period of cultic sacrifice is completely over, for now God is well pleased by the sacrifice of our body. For Paul, the offering of the body was the same as offering the total person. In this regard he was thinking of man as belonging to the world and of his God-given ability to communicate, as well as his bodily existence and his ability to love. "God lays claim to our bodily existence because he is no longer leaving the world to its own course. In the obedience of our bodily existence one perceives that God is calling the world to which we belong, in and through us back to his service." In following Jesus "the teaching of worship falls necessarily together with Christian ethics" [55.200-201].

The everyday world—in the midst of which one finds the gathering of the church—is the actual forum of spiritual worship. The gospel of God's love in Jesus Christ and the command to love are its liturgy. Its festive content is the experience of my acceptance and the communication that is achieved with the lost and the solidarity with the weak. The life of the Christian is an ongoing fest, because it integrates the everyday world and is open to one's neighbors [58.755]. Worship in the everyday world is a part of following Jesus. One is not spared disruptive experiences; thus, he needs Jesus' quiet certainty to safeguard the joy of discipleship.

XI. Joy in Suffering

Jesus' proclamation brought about opposition; his conduct led to confrontations with the religious and political representatives of the time. His way was characterized by hostility, persecution, and suffering; he ended up on a cross. The word of the prophet who "is not without honor but in his own town" (Mark 6:4, par.) points in that direction as well. This is also the case in the tradition found in Luke 13:31-33, which at its core is very authentic. There a Pharisee came to Jesus and warned him:

> Get out, and depart hence; for Herod will kill you. And he said, "Go and tell that fox, Behold I cast out devils, and I do cures today and tomorrow . . . and on the following day, I must walk, for it cannot be that a prophet perish out of Jerusalem." [10:142]

Jesus was able, and indeed had, to reckon with his death. Luke 13:33 indicates that Jesus saw his function under the influence of the characteristic picture of the violent fate of the prophets. There was a different interpretation given to it after Easter [86.183]. Jesus called disciples to follow him and encouraged them to share his fate. Discipleship is joy (*cf.* chapter 9); however, (the Jesus tradition does not cover it over) it means that factually one must experience separation from house and family (Luke 14:26) and difficult wandering from village to village, homelessness (Matt. 8:20) and a radical existence of wandering [103, *passim*], strife, hostility, indeed persecution, and possible death.

> Think not that I am come to send peace to earth; I came not to send peace, but a sword. (Matt. 10:34)
> Whoever does not take up his cross and follow me cannot be my disciple. (Luke 14:27)
> No man, having put his hand to the plough and looking back, is fit for the kingdom of God. (Luke 9:62)

Suffering is joyless, for pain, sadness, and fear belong in its circle, then as well as today. These statements about the suffering of Jesus set forth that truth even though they were formulated in the post-Easter church, a church that was very conscious and determined to follow the way of the cross (*cf.* only Mark 8:31, 9:31, 10:33-34, par.). Yet this same church passed on the tradition of the prayer struggle in Gethsemane (Mark 14:32-34, par.) and the cry of dereliction (Mark 15:34, par.).

The writer of the book of Hebrews appears to have these experiences in mind when he says that Jesus "in the days of his flesh, when he had offered up prayers and supplications with strong crying and tears unto God was set free from his fear" (Heb. 5:7). He also knew of the experience of suffering that was a part of the chastening found in the Old Testament. "To be sure, *for the present* chastening does not seem to be joyous, but rather painful" *but afterward* it yields the peaceable fruit of righteousness (12:4 ff, better, verse 11). Accordingly it can be said of Jesus that "who for the joy that was set before him endured the cross despising the shame" (Heb. 12:2). Suffering and joy stand closely together in this formulation, but they are not one and the same. Suffering remains a "painful subject"; joy must follow after it.

This apparently paradoxical thought of *joy in suffering* runs on through other statements concerning suffering as a part of following Jesus. The beatitude praising the persecuted (Matt. 5:11-12) speaks of this:

I*a*:   Blessed are you,
I*b*:   when men shall revile you, and persecute you, and shall say all manner of evil against you falsely, for my sake.
II*a*:   Rejoice and be exceeding glad;
II*b*:   for great is your reward in heaven; (for so persecuted they the prophets which were before you).

This same thought is met also in I Peter and the Letter of James. I Peter 4:12-14: "Beloved, think it not strange concerning the ficry trial which is to try you, as though some strange thing happened unto you. But *rejoice* (= IIa) inasmuch as you are partakers of Christ's suffering; that, *when his glory shall be revealed, you may be glad also with exceeding joy* (= IIb). *If you be reproached* (= Ib) *for the name of Christ, happy are you* (= Ia) for the spirit of glory and of God rests upon you." I Peter 1:3-6 (= IIb): "For you is laid up in heaven an inheritance incorruptible; *wherein you greatly rejoice*, IIa though now for a season, if need be, *you are grieving because* of *manifold temptations* (= Ib)." James 1:12: "*Blessed is the man* (Ia) *who endures temptations* (Ib); *for when he is tried he shall receive the crown of life* (IIb) which the Lord has promised to them that love him." James 1:2:"*Brethren count it all joy* (IIa) *when you fall into all kinds of temptations* (Ib).

The quoted texts all follow the same basic scheme: Ia, the call ("salvation"); Ib, the condition ("persecution"); IIa, the summons ("joy"); IIb, the foundation ("reward"). There are also remarkable parallels in the detailed facets as well. The direct literary dependence between the beatitude of persecution, which can be traced back to the Q source, and the passages from I Peter and James leads one to conclude with some certainty that there was an early Christian persecution tradition, which in form and motif asserted that there was "joy in suffering." Other New Testament passages, though thoroughly colored, are also found in this tradition [78.68-73]. For example, Hebrews 10:32 reminds the readers of their "struggle of suffering."

> For you had compassion on me in my bonds and *took joyfully* the spoiling of your goods, knowing in yourselves that you have in heaven a better and an enduring substance. Cast not away, therefore, your confidence, which has great recompense of reward. (Heb. 10:34-35)

In Acts 5:41 the motif "joy in suffering" has been sharpened to "joy concerning suffering." There it is said of the apostles that they departed *joyfully* *"because they had been counted worthy to suffer shame for his name." Paul also recognized the paradoxical synopsis of joy and suffering. That thought had great significance for him (cf.* page 191 ff).

The thought of joy in suffering is not genuinely Christian, but is also evident in Judaism. It belongs within the tradition of the suffering of the righteous, which in turn had overcome the older concept of a deed-result relationship (*cf.* page 82). It marks a breakthrough to a new theological perception. Here beatitudes and shouts of joy exist in the present tense beside statements of suffering and the promise of future salvation [101.254 ff]. One should also take notice of the Syrian Apocalypse of Baruch, chapters 48:48-50 and 52:2-7 and 54:16-18 where "all four points of the New Testament outline are found" in the same order as Matthew 5:11-12, par. [78:75-76].

   I*a*:   (48:49)   I will relate to you (the righteous salvation.
   I*b*:   (48:50)   You have suffered much trouble (difficulty).
   II*a*:   (52:6)   Rejoice in the suffering in which you now suffer.
   II*b*:   (52:7)   Prepare yourselves for that which has already been made ready for you and for the reward which is laid up for you.

The tradition concerning joy in suffering came into existence in the first third of the second century B.C. in the massive threats and persecution that the pious of Israel experienced. After the victory of Antiochus III over Ptolemy V in the battle of Panium in 198 B.C., Palestine came under the control of Syrian power and an increased Hellenistic influence. In I Maccabees 1:11-13 it is related that such an influence was welcomed by some in Israel, especially among the leading circles of priests and nobles. These people said, "We want to establish an agreement with these friendly people who live around us; for ever since we were set apart from them, it has not gone well with us" (I Macc. 1:11).

As a consequence of this concept a gymnasium was built in
Jerusalem and the young Jewish athletes allowed the sign of
Israel, circumcision, to be removed from their bodies—a clear
indication of the decline of the covenant (I Macc. 1:14-15). An
open conflict developed as Antiochus IV Epiphanes [175–164,
163] decided to force the Hellenization that had already begun.
A rigorous politics of religion would give to his kingdom a
unified order of life and cult and end the religious life of Israel.
First Maccabees 1:44-50 gives an indication of the significance
of that policy:

> (The Jews) shall adopt the foreign customs. Burnt offerings,
> sacrifices, and drink offerings were to be discontinued;
> sabbaths and festivals were profaned; the holy places and
> holy things were disgraced. Instead of these, they were
> required to erect altars, holy places, and temples for foreign
> gods, as well as offer up sacrifices of swine and other unclean
> animals. They were not allowed to circumcise their
> sons . . . and by this means, it was hoped that the law would
> soon be forgotten and all of its requirements would fall into
> disuse. Whoever did not follow these instructions would
> surely die.

Antiochus disgraced and robbed the temple in Jerusalem. In
fact, a foreign temple was erected on Mount Zion in honor of the
Zeus Olympus cult; the temple on Mount Gerizim was made a
holy place for Zeus Xenios. In this way the first commandment
was put in jeopardy and Israel's very existence was placed in
question. Such provocation brought about the resistance of the
scattered pious and constituted the beginning point of a
political and religious revival. In the so-called Maccabean
rebellion the pious enjoyed the protection of Yahweh, and
there were astonishing victories of the Maccabeans against the
Seleucid troops. In 164 B.C. the temple in Jerusalem was
rededicated to the worship of Yahweh. However, the pious of
Israel also experienced over and over again their painful

powerlessness, when they were visited by the overseers and officials of the king who came to the small villages to enforce the royal commands. The only possible way of remaining loyal to Yahweh was to face martyrdom. Suffering in holy wars for Yahweh against gentile opposition was viewed as the only conscientious course of action. Such suffering was considered to be a trial, just as the patriarchs had been put to the test by God, and not punishment. Such a trial was something for which to give thanks (Jdt 8:25-27; compare I Peter 4:12-13). The pious were thoroughly filled with the hope that they would enjoy a great blessing after their short period of chastisement was over. God was only putting them to the test and would bless them for their perseverance (Wisd. of Sol. 3:4-6). In this connection we find the words concerning the pious' joy of suffering in the struggle against the commands of Antiochus. A good example of this is found in the sixth chapter of II Maccabees in the story of the old man Eleazar who said as he died: "With all of his holy knowledge, the Lord knows that I was able to escape death; my body suffered terribly under the blows, my soul, however, bore it *with joy* because I feared him" (verse 6:30).

The insights achieved under the extreme conditions of the Maccabean wars, such as joy in suffering, were retained and developed. This is shown in the texts cited above from the Apocalypse of Baruch and from the New Testament. This motif is also found in rabbinical Judaism and at Qumran. In both places it is possible to set forth with assurance the connection of the tradition to the pious of the second century B.C. who were devoted to the law. At Qumran it could be said:

> For you my God . . . direct my struggles; for in the secret of your wisdom you have shown me the right way. . . . *And your directions are a joy* and a delight and healing to my wounds . . . and the contempt of my enemy becomes a crown of honor and my failures are turned into eternal strength. (1 QH IX, 23-25)

In rabbinical Judaism we find the formula, "If you desire life, then look forward to chastisement" and "It is salvation to the righteous when the plight in this world is the same as that which the godless will receive in the next." (For: "God is very particular with both groups. He is particular with the righteous and drives punishment from them for the few evil deeds which they have committed in this world and grants them a good reward in the future. In the same way, he gives rich goodness and well-being to the godless in this world and repays their few good works in this world with punishment in the future.") [7, II. 278; I. 390]

Those who are oppressed (the humiliated) and who do not return the same, those who listen to abuse without responding to it, those who act out of love (to God) and *rejoice in suffering* may hear the words of Judges 5:31: "Those who love him are as the rising of the sun in full power" [7,I. 226]. "Everyone who *rejoices over his suffering* brings salvation into the world." [Gen. R. 84.1003]

Early Christianity took up the thought of joy in suffering as it experienced rejection and persecution in its mission to Israel. These experiences were freely related to the beatitude praising the persecuted (Matt. 5:11-12, par.) or to the experience of martyrdom of individual righteous ones, such as Stephen (Acts 7), James, son of Zebedee (Acts 12:2), the Lord's brother James (Josephus, Ant. XX. 200), Peter and Paul, or the persecution of the church in Rome under Nero, or especially in the great Christian persecution in the last decade of the first century under Caesar Domitian, which formed the background for I Peter. Here the phrase "joy in suffering" was joined to the Christian movement; in that the suffering of Jesus was linked to the suffering on his behalf, whoever suffers on his behalf is blessed. This promise of salvation is even stronger than the tradition of late Judaism and is made even sharper for the present: now in suffering and in spite of suffering, the time of salvation has dawned [78.76].

Paul understood and accepted the suffering of his churches and his own suffering as a "making present" of the Crucified One. Christian existence for him was taking on the cross of Christ and to be "in Christ" meant to die with Christ and be resurrected with him. The sharing in the suffering of Christ is the strongest concrete experienceable proof for the fact that one is a living member of the Body of Christ and that one is thereby granted the resurrection power of this body [34, I. 230]. This shared suffering is a reason for joy, because it makes the resurrection certain; suffering in joy presumes resurrection joy.

In this sense Paul wrote the newly founded church at Thessalonica that just like the churches in Judea (I Thess. 2:14; 3:3-4) its faith had been proven through persecution:

> Knowing brethren, beloved, your election of God. For our gospel came not in word only but also in power, and in the Holy Spirit, and in much assurance as you know what manner of men we were among you for your sake. *And you became followers of us, and of the Lord, having received the word in much affliction with joy of the Holy Spirit;* so that you became examples to all that believe in Macedonia and Achaia. (I Thess. 1:4-7)

In the Corinthian correspondence Paul made use of the example of the Macedonian churches. The Corinthians should remember that example as they gathered the collection for the poor Christians in Jerusalem. For Paul that served as a good example of "sharing in suffering." "We would like to report to you, brothers, of the grace of God bestowed on the churches of Macedonia. *How that in a great trial* of *affliction* the *abundance of their joy* and their deep poverty abounded unto the riches of their liberality" (II Cor. 8:1-2).

This verse, which almost explodes with force, sets one paradox next to another: "deepest poverty" is expressed in "richest giving"; in the midst of many tests of suffering, there is an excess of joy. Paul experienced his own course in the service of the gospel in a similar way; he was once, as he said, "a persecutor of the church of God" (Gal. 1:13), but now as one persecuted, he had suffered a great deal of pain. Pressed by his opponents, he would relate that he was an apostle; he was a servant of Christ even as they or even more than they, as his suffering "proved."

> Are they ministers of Christ? . . . I am more; in labors more abundant, in stripes above measure, in prisons more frequent, in deaths oft. Of the Jews five times received I forty stripes save one. Three times I was beaten with rods, once was I stoned, three times I suffered shipwreck, a night and a day I have been in the deep; in journeyings often, in perils of wars, in perils of robbers, in perils of mine own countrymen, in perils by the heathen, in perils in the city, in perils in the wilderness, in perils in the sea, in perils among false brethren; in weariness and painfulness, in watchings often, in hunger and thirst, in fastings often, in cold and nakedness. (II Cor. 11:23-27)

This (incomplete) narrative is very powerful; yet Paul in his suffering did not give in or become dumbfounded. He rather accepted it in faith and for that reason was "happy all the time" (II Cor. 6:10) as freely receiving it from God's hand. Suffering for him was suffering in the sorrows of Jesus Christ (Phil. 3:10); it linked him with Christ and at the same time with all fellow Christians in the Body of Christ (I Cor. 12:25-26). Indeed, Paul bore the "wounds" (Gal. 6:17) and the "death of Christ" in his own body in the hope and believing assurance that in the same way the life of Christ would be manifest in his mortal body (II Cor. 4:10-11). And the apostle also understood that suffering made him aware of his weakness; it taught and reminded and pressed him always not to rely on his own strength, not to be "spared" but rather to comprehend his own existence as a gift (of grace), including his own serious illness against which he often remonstrated, only to hear the Lord say to him:

"My grace is sufficient for you; for my strength is made perfect in weakness." Most gladly, therefore, will I rather glory in my infirmities, that the power of Christ may rest upon me. Therefore, I take pleasure in infirmities, in reproaches, in necessities, in persecutions, in distresses for Christ's sake; for when I am weak, then am I strong. (II Cor. 12:9b-10)

The power of Christ that is the subject here makes one free and calm. It grants independence and security at the end. Paul experienced this and formulated it in the following antitheses:

We are troubled on every side, yet not distressed; we are perplexed, but not in despair. (II Cor. 4:8)

Being reviled, we bless; being persecuted, we suffer it; (I Cor. 4:12b)

As the ministers of God, in much patience, in afflictions, in necessities, in distresses . . . by pureness, by knowledge, by long suffering, . . . by love unfeigned. By the word of truth, by the power of God, by the armor of righteousness on the right hand and on the left, by honor and dishonor, by evil report and good report, as deceivers, and yet true; as unknown, and yet well known; as dying, and behold, we live; as chastened, and not killed; as sorrowful, *yet always rejoicing*; as poor, yet making many rich; as having nothing, and yet possessing all things. (II Cor. 6:4-10)

Here the existence of the believer is described in an absolute sense; the perception of the world is always at once the perception of the love of God. He is convinced and assured that nothing—life nor death—can separate him from the love of God (Rom. 8:38-39) and that "all things work together for good for those that love God" (Rom. 8:28). Whoever lives in this faith loses his fear of death and sorrow; they are overcome in faith; "the joy of the Lord" (Phil. 3:1; 4:4) need not be silenced. The Philippian Letter is a moving document of such faith, a letter of joy that grows out of great sorrow.

Paul found himself (once again) in prison (Phil. 1:7, 13, 17), probably in Ephesus. His arrest became a "sign" for him; it served the advance of the gospel, for everyone knew that he was in prison not as a criminal but as a Christian missionary. This imprisonment caused the brethren to increase their courage in fruitful preaching; there was, of course, rivalry but that made no difference as long as Christ was proclaimed. Concerning this, Paul said, *"I rejoice"* (Phil. 1:12-18).

The judicial process had not finished its course; it could end in life or death. Yet Paul would accept either in joy:

> *And I will rejoice.* For I know that this shall turn to my salvation through your prayers and the supply of the Spirit of Jesus Christ according to my earnest expectation and my hope, that in nothing I shall be ashamed, but that with all boldness, as always, so now also Christ shall be magnified in my body, whether it be by life or by death. For to me to live is Chist and to die is gain. (Phil. 1:19-21)
> Yes, and if I be offered up on the sacrifice and service of your faith, *I joy and rejoice with you all.* (Phil. 2:17)

Paul could say of himself, "For I have the desire to depart and to be with Christ" (Phil. 1:23). However, he did not seek martyrdom, for the missionary effort needed him. It meant "furtherance and joy of faith" (Phil. 1:25) for the Philippians (and others) just as the church, carrying out its life under the command to love, was his "joy and his (glory) crown" and filled Paul with joy (Phil. 2:2; 4:1). The one imprisoned (Paul) was a living proof of joy in suffering and invited all to an overwhelming joy.

> Finally, my brethren, *rejoice in the Lord.* (Phil. 3:1a)
> *Rejoice in the Lord alway*, and again I say, *rejoice.* Let your moderation be known unto all men. The Lord is at hand. Be careful for nothing; but in everything, by prayer and supplication with thanksgiving, let your requests be made known unto God. And the peace of God which passes

all understanding shall keep your hearts and minds through
Christ Jesus. (Phil. 4:4-7)

Joy belongs as love (friendliness) to the special characteristics of
the existence of a Christian (Gal. 5:22-23). The essence of the
kingdom of God consists, indeed as is indicated in Romans 14:17,
"in righteousness, peace, and *joy* through the Holy Spirit" and
the believer has a share in faith; he is "rejoicing in hope" (Rom.
12:12); his being is "an eschatological being, a being in joy"
[16.340-41], independent of external conditions and without
temporal limitations, "Rejoice in the Lord *alway*" (Phil. 4:4).

Where there is worry, there cannot be joy; for this reason
Paul in his call to joy termed the lack of worry as a further sign of
the Christian life-style. "Worry about nothing" (Phil. 4:6). This
exhortation takes up a word of Jesus' proclamation. It reminds
us of the quiet certainty of Jesus and makes certain the faith
and the joy of his church:

> Do not take concern for your life. . . . Behold the birds of
> the air. They neither sow nor neither do they reap, nor
> gather into barns; yet your heavenly Father feeds them. Are
> you not much better than they? . . . Consider the lilies of
> the field, how they grow; they toil not, neither do they spin;
> and yet I say unto you, that even Solomon in all his glory was
> not arrayed like one of these. (Matt. 6:25-29)

In an extreme situation, Paul gave an example of such lack of
worry; he rejoiced abundantly even in sorrow and invited
others to this joy. The joy was not some heroic accomplishment
but a gift experienced in faith; he was able to do all through the
One who strengthened him (Phil. 4:12-13).

Joy in suffering, as we can finally conclude, is absolute
Christian joy. It came with Jesus into the world and is not
forgotten even in the shadow of the cross. Joy in suffering
"realizes" that God stands by the poor and the lost and wants to
save them.

The confession "Jesus is there even in sorrow, Jesus my joy" turns one's glance to faith; "the strength of the one now believing" is stressed and at the same time made more certain [99.202]. The call to joy in suffering is not at all a glorification of suffering. It sets forth the fact that God's love resists suffering, for he is near even in suffering. The nearness of God, which suffered in the cross of Jesus, brings salvation for suffering humanity. Joy in suffering, as an expression of the faith existence of Christianity, signifies already a share in the final joy that will beam forth when God wipes away all tears from every eye and death is no more and there is no suffering (Rev. 21:4).

NOTES

1. Haag (35.67 ff), more cautiously Laaf (70.89), would like to see the mention of Gilgal in Joshua 5:10-12 eliminated, although he views it as very old in its basic form. It is evident that already in Joshua 4:19b it is said that the Israelites camped at Gilgal. Yet Joshua 4:19b and Joshua 5:10 belong to different literary connections.

The Matzoth Festival had its origin in the Israel of the land of culture. Thus any dependency on a Canaanite harvest festival is doomed to failure due to the dating; the first of Abib, which I consider to be the most likely date for the beginning of the Matzoth Festival, came too early for any consideration of relating it to the grain harvest. In addition, the commands concerning the observance of Matzoth in Exodus 23 and Exodus 34, in contrast to the rules concerning the Festival of Weeks and the festival of ingathering, give no indication of any agrarian connection. Much more essential for the Matzoth Festival was the taking of the land and the relation to Exodus [81.186 ff, 296 ff]. This shows that the Matzoth Festival was formulated in the framework of the Israelite tribes in the land of culture in which Gilgal took on enormous significance. In this regard we have to reckon with a blending of various motifs. Thus, the adoption of the *heilsgeschichtlichen* themes of the taking of the land and Exodus was very important. In the Matzoth ritual of the unleavened bread, we encounter a custom which goes back to the unleavened bread of the nomads which was eaten just before setting forth. In Joshua 5:10-12 we find no recognizable connection to the harvest of the land, which in turn was related to the offering of the first born in the Matzoth Festival. Here a Canaanite agrarian motif has been adopted which can be explained from the desire of taking away from the Canaanite the responsibility for the gods of fertility of the land and in turn attributing it to Yahweh.

I do not agree with Halbe [38.324 ff] in seeing the origin of the Matzoth ritual in the Passover. There is no pre-Deuteronomic proof that Matzah bread was eaten in the course of the Passover before it was connected with the Matzoth Festival. In Joshua 5:10-12, according to Halbe, the Passover theme in its linguistic construction is secondary; for Joshua 5:10-12 in its subject matter is hardly an original Passover tradition, since it contains no typical Passover motif but rather possesses only those belonging to the Matzoth Festival. Thus Joshua 5:10-12 is not a support for the tendency found in Deuteronomy 16 of replacing the Passover with the Matzoth Festival, but rather demonstrates the tendency of linking the two together as found in Deuteronomy 16. Even in Exodus 12 the themes of Passover and Matzoth have been redactionally joined together [83.3 ff].

2. Compare also Kraus [65.181 ff]; Soggin [100.263 ff]; Wilcoxen [112.43 ff].

3. This does not contradict, however, the notice found in Joshua 3:15b, "The Jordan River during the harvest season overflowed all its banks," since it was added to source B in the steps of the development of Deuteronomy. It is the concern there to show the miraculous nature of the crossing of the Jordan. Since the Matzoth Festival fell on the first of Abib, in the middle of our March, it would not be bothered by the high water of April.

4. Compare also the enumeration of the tribes in the song of Deborah, Judges 5. There is no indication during the time of the Judges of the tribe of Judah participating in any combined action with the other tribes of Israel. Finally, none of the tradition which predates the twelve tribes is older than the time of Saul with the exception of that related to Gilgal [cf. 81.322 ff].

5. It should be emphasized that in no way should Gilgal be characterized as an "amphictyony-holy place." One can demonstrate that the development of the idea of Judah's belonging to the other tribes had only a regional significance and was unknown elsewhere as is shown in Judges 5 [85.165 ff].

6. For further historical background on the Davidic foreign affairs and religious politics, see 84.65 ff.

7. For more on the Hebrew root *saedaeq* which has lost most of its meaning and thus is poorly translated as "righteous," see von Rad [89. I: 382 ff]. It would be better characterized as a salvific community relationship.

8. The motif of the "battle of the nations" is found most convincingly in the Jebusite tradition in Jerusalem [102.72 ff or 86 ff]; Von Rad does not agree [89, II. 162 ff]. For a cultic interpretation of political relationships in Egypt, see 44:9 ff.

9. The concept of the mountain of God is also connected to the El-Berith of Shechem [cf. Judges 9:37; for Bethel, cf. Gen. 28:11 ff; and also 85.165-66].

10. Verse 1 is made up of comments added later.

11. The cry of proclamation is to be distinguished from the enthronement cry and acclamation cry.

12. This syntactical structure of the formula—a verbal statement in Psalm 47—gives us no reason to bring into question the motif of enthronement; Kraus thinks otherwise [67.202-3].

13. Even in the David-Solomon period the ark of the covenant was established in Jerusalem [81.199 ff], and it is quite probable that a celebration was held in honor of the establishment of the covenant up until the time of the divided monarchy.

14. For the linguistic background of joy *(śimha)* in Hebrew, see 39.1333-34. In contrast ritualistic crying in reaction to a dying God was excluded because Yahweh was not understood as a dying and rising God [*cf.* 46.185 ff].

15. According to this view, this condition is not related to Yahweh's judgment in the sense of recompense for a deed. Much more the deed had a direct impact on the one committing it, in that it established around him a sphere of salvation or destruction which determined his condition. Since a sphere of destruction involved a threat for the whole community and an evil deed also had social implications, the community could level sanctions that led even unto death [*cf.* 59.1-2].

16. Koch [63.217-18] has shown that the thought of a divine forgiveness in the sense that the deed-result relationship lost its power may not have played a role in the preexilic period. In the prophetic pleas, it was always a matter of calling for the weakening not the absolvement of this relationship.

17. The mythical motif of the Jerusalem cult was suppressed in P [*cf.* 61.99].

18. Verse 1 is a doublet to verse 2 and as such a literary addition to the P source (g) and serves as a bridge to Leviticus 10. In any case, the conclusion of the tradition has been extended literarily by verses 29-34*a*, in that vocabulary and style in the second person plural set it apart from its context. In this way the literary additions to P(g) are exhausted so that the main weight of the development of the traditio-historical primitive period of the sources and their redaction rests on P. The ritualistic tradition, which dates before the primitive written source, begins with verse 4b: "And he washed himself with water and dressed himself." Verse 23 requires the removal of the linen clothing at the conclusion of the ritual so that it could be included again in the act of putting on clothing. The comparison with verse 23 demonstrates beyond that, that P has extended this element by an exact description of the clothing. Thus, verse 4 originally read: "Then he put on the linen clothing." It is also apparent in this context that verse 4 breaks the context with verses 3 and 5. Verse 4b is then extended by P into verse 4ab. "Clothing made from linen" was eliminated by P in favor of a full narrative. Thus the difficulty in verse 4 where Aaron bathes his body after he has just put on the priestly garments can be explained as the redaction of P. Verses 5, 10, 17*a*, 25 evolve as imperfectly formed sentences *(formgeschichtlich)* out of a connection with the ritualistic tradition. The offering of the priestly bullock has been introduced here by P from Leviticus 4. Originally, it was only an offering of a goat for Yahweh and the expulsion of the one for Azazel. This was done to make clear that also the priests needed to make atonement for themselves on the Day of Atonement. Thus, verses 16, 11, 14 are an addition from the redactional priestly source to the prepriestly ritualistic tradition. The extension of the atonement for the holy place to include the priests, their families, and all of Israel found in verse 17 is to be attributed in any case to the redaction of P. In verse 19*a* the atonement ritual, which originally was related only to the most holy places, was extended to sprinkling blood on the altar. In this way P stressed the corporate nature of

Israel's sins through the adding of verses 16ab, 21a. In verses 24b and 25 the idea of the preparation of a burnt offering as an extension of verses 3, 5 is clearly an addition, in order to stress the thought of atonement after the driving out of the goat designated for Azazel in the form of a sacrifice. In this way the sacrificial rites constitute much more the framework of the rituals. In verses 26a and 28, P has taken over the apodictic command for the Day of Atonement, which should be separated (formgeschichtlich) from the ritual tradition. These related to the cultic purification of persons who had become impure through the rituals [61.95-96]. The conclusion of the presource ritual tradition is in verse 27: "And the goat for the sin offering was brought out of the camp and his flesh burned with fire."

19. Rendtorff's analysis [92.59 ff], which sees in verses 11, 14/15, 16 and verses 20b, 21 three originally independent rituals, contradicts the fact that verse 15 is not a doublet, but rather a continuation of verse 9. Corresponding to the supposed ritual, verses 11, 14, the introductory and concluding verses are missing. Also, Rendtorff must grasp for the thesis that the second ritual, verses 15-16, came into being independent of that in verse 11, 14. What can be said in favor of these limitations?

20. In his earliest form, Azazel must have been a desert demon [cf. Enoch VI, 8 ff 69; cf. 104, II. 370]. Rost [93.212 ff] places the Azazel ritual along with the Passover ritual in the connection of a change of pasture and thus views it as an offering to the desert demon during the winter wandering from the land of culture into the desert. Rost replaces the blood ritual, which stems from another religionsgeschichtliche context, the cleansing of a holy place, to this context of changing of the pastures.

Bibliography

1. Alt, A., Der Gott der Väter, Alt I, pp. 1-78.

2. ———. Erwägungen über die Landnahme der Israeliten in Palästina, Alt I, pp. 126-75; English Translation; hereafter to be designated as E.T., Essays on Old Testament History and Religion, 1967, pp. 173-221.

3. ———. Die Staatenbildung der Israeliten in Palästina, Alt II, pp. 1-65; E.T., Essays on Old Testament History and Religion, 1967, pp. 223-309.

4. Bauer, W., Der Wortgottesdienst der ältesten Christen, 1930.

5. Baumgartner, H., "Ugaritische Probleme und ihre Tragweite für das Alte Testament," ThZ 3, 1947, pp. 87-100.

6. Becker, J., *Johannes der Täufer und Jesus von Nazareth*, 1972.

7. Billerbeck, P., and Strack, H.L., *Kommentar zum Neuen Testament aus Talmud und Midrasch*, I-IV, 1922-28.

8. Billerbeck, P., "Ein Tempelgottesdienst in Jesu Tagen," *ZNW* 55, 1964, pp. 1-17.

9. ———. "Ein Synagogengottesdienst in Jesu Tagen," *ZNW* 55, 1964, pp. 143-61.

10. Bornkamm, G., *Jesus von Nazareth*, 1960; E.T., *Jesus of Nazareth*, 1975.

11. ———. *Paulus*, 1969; E.T., *Paul*, 1971.

12. ———. "Zum Verständnis des Gottesdienstes bei Paulus," *Das Ende des Gesetzes. Paulusstudien, Ges. Aufs*, I⁴, 1963, pp. 113-32.

13. Braun, H., *Jesus*, 1969.

14. Bultmann, R., *Jesus*, 1926; E.T., *Jesus and the Word*, 1934.

15. ———. *Die Geschichte der synoptischen Tradition*, ⁵ 1961; E.T., *The History of the Synoptic Tradition*, 1968.

16. ———. *Theologie des Neuen Testaments*, ⁴ 1961; E.T., *The Theology of the New Testament*, 2 vols., 1951-55.

17. ———. "Optimismus und Pessimismus in Antike und Christentum," *Glaube und Verstehen* IV, 1965, pp. 69-90.

18. Conrad, H., *Studien zum Altargesetz Ex. 20:24-26*, 1968.

19. Cox, H., *Das Fest der Narren*, ⁴1972; E.T., *Feast of Fools*, 1972.

20. Degengardt, H. J., *Lukas-Evangelist der Armen*, 1965.

21. Delling, G., *Der Gottesdienst im Neuen Testament*, 1952; E.T., *Worship in the New Testament*, 1962.

22. Dibelius, M., and Kümmel, W. G., *Jesus*, 1966; E.T., *Jesus*, 1949.

23. Du Toit, A.D., *Der Aspekt der Freude im urchristlichen Abendmahl*, 1965.

24. Eichholz, G., *Auslegung der Bergpredigt*, 1965.
25. Elbogen, I., *Der jüdische Gottesdienst in seiner geschichtlichen Entwicklung*, ³ 1931.
26. Engnell, I., "Paesah-massot and the Problem of 'Patternism,'" *Orientalia Suenica* 1, 1952, pp. 39-50.
27. Fiedler, P., *Jesus und die Sünder*, 1976.
28. Flusser, D., *Jesus*, 1968; E.T., *Jesus*, 1967.
29. Friedrich, G., "Evangelium etc," *ThWNT*, II, pp. 705-37; E.T., "Evangelium," TDNT, II, pp. 707-37.
30. Gaster, T. H., *Thespis. Ritual, Myth, and Drama in the Ancient Near East*, 1950.
31. Gese, H., "Die Religion Altsyriens," *Die Religionen der Menschheit*, 10.2, 1970.
32. Gollwitzer, H., *Die Freude Gottes. Einführung in das Lukasevangelium*, o.J.
33. Grundmann, W., *Das Evangelium nach Matthäus*, 1968.
34. Gulin, E. G., *Die Freude im Neuen Testament* I/II, 1932.
35. Haag, H., *Vom alten zum neuen Pascha*, 1971.
36. Hahn, F., *Christologische Hoheitstitel*, 1963; E.T., *The Titles of Jesus in Christology*, 1966.
37. ———. *Der urchristliche Gottesdienst*, 1970; E.T., *The Worship of the Early Church*, 1975.
38. Halbe, J., "Erwägungen zu Ursprung und Wesen des Mazzotfestes," ZAW 87, 1975, pp. 324-46.
39. Hamp, V., *Die Wurzel Samach im AT*, WZ Halle-Wittenberg. Gesellsch. and Sprachwiss. Reihe 10.2, 1961, pp. 1333-34.
40. Henniger, J., "Les fetes de printemps chez les Arabes et leurs implications historiques," *Rivista do Museo Paulista* 4, 1950, pp. 389-432.
41. Herrmann, S., *Geschichte Israels in alttestamentlicher Zeit*, 1973.

42. Hirsch, L., *Jüdische Glaubenwelt*, 1962.
43. Hoffmann, P., and Eid, V., *Jesus von Nazareth und eine christliche Moral*, 1975.
44. Hornung, E., *Geschichte als Fest*, 1966.
45. Hübner, H., *Das Gesetz in der synoptischen Tradition*, 1973.
46. Hvidberg, F. F., *Weeping and Laughter in the Old Testament*, 1962.
47. Jaussen, A., *Coutumes des Arabes au pays de Moab*, ²1948.
48. Jeremias, J., *Jesus als Weltvollender*, 1930.
49. ———. *Die Abendmahlsworte Jesu*, ³1960; E.T., *The Eucharistic Words of Jesus*, 1977.
50. ———. *Die Gleichnisse Jesus*, ⁶1962; E.T., *The Parables of Jesus*, 1955.
51. ———. *Neutestamentliche Theologie* I. Die Verkündung Jesus, 1971; E.T., *New Testament Theology* I. The Proclamation of Jesus, 1971.
52. Jülicher, A., *Die Gleichnisreden Jesu*, I/II, 1899.
53. Jüngel, E., *Paulus und Jesus*, ²1964.
54. Käsemann, E., "Das Problem des historischen Jesus," *Exegetische Versuche und Besinnungen* I, 1964, pp. 187-214; E.T., *Essays on New Testament Themes*, 1964.
55. ———. "Gottesdienst im Alltag der Welt," *Exegetische Versuche und Besinnungen* II, 1965, pp. 198-204; E.T., *New Testament Questions of Today*, 1969, p. 188.
56. Keel, O., "Erwägungen zum Sitz im Leben des vormasaischen Pascha und zur Etymologie von Pesah," *ZAW* 84, 1972, pp. 414-34.
57. Kenyon, K., *Digging Up Jericho*, 1957.
58. Klausner, Th., "Art. Fest," *RAC* VII, pp. 747-66.
59. Koch, K., "Gibt es ein Vergeltungsdogma im Alten Testament?" *ZThK* 52, 1955, pp. 1-42.
60. ———. "Die Eigenart der priesterschriftlichen Sinaigesetzgebung," *ZThK* 55, 1958, pp. 36-51.

61. ———. *Die Priesterschrift von Exodus 25–Leviticus 16*, 1959.

62. ———. "Wesen und Ursprung der Gemeinschaftstreue im Israel der Königzeit," *ZEE* 5, 1961, pp. 72-90.

63. ———. "Sühne und Sündenvergebung um die Wende von der exilischen und nachexilischen Zeit," *EvTh* 26, 1966, pp. 217-39.

64. ———. "Die Entstehung der sozialen Kritik bei den Profeten," *Probleme biblischer Theologie. Festschrift v. Rad*, 1971, pp. 236-57.

65. Kraus, H. J., "Gilgal. Ein Beitrag zur Kultgeschichte Israels," *VT* 1, 1951, pp. 181-99.

66. ———. "Gottesdienst im alten und neuen Bund," *EvTh*, 25, 1965, pp. 171-206.

67. ———. *Psalmen*, Biblischer Kommentar 15, ³1966.

68. ———. *Geschichte der historisch-kritischen Erforschung des Alten Testaments*, ²1969.

69. Kümmel, W. G., *Verheissung und Erfüllung. Untersuchungen zur eschatologischen Verkündigung Jesu*, ³1956; E.T., *Promise and Fulfillment*, 1957.

70. Laaf, P., *Die Pascha-Feier Israels*, 1970.

71. Lohse, E., "Jesus Worte über den Sabbat," *Judentum-Urchristentum-Kirche*," Festschrift Jeremias, 1960, pp. 79-93.

72. ———. "Sabbat," *ThWNt* VII, pp. 1-35; E.T., "Sabbath," *TDNT*, pp. 1-35.

73. Michel, D. *Tempora und Satzstellung in den Psalmen*, 1960.

74. Michel, O., "Freude," *RAC* VIII, pp. 348-418.

75. Mowinckel, E., *Psalmenstudien* I-IV, 1922-24; E.T., *The Psalms in Israel's Worship*, 2 vols., 1963.

76. ———. *Religion und Kultus*, 1953.

77. Müller, H. P., *Mythos, Tradition, Revolution*, 1973.

78. Nauck, W., "Freude im Leiden. Zum Problem einer

urchristlichen Verfolgung stradition," *ZNW* 46, 1955, pp. 68-80.

79. Noth, M., *Überlieferungsgeschichte des Pentateuch*, 1948; E.T., *A History of Pentateuchal Traditions*, 1972.

80. ———. *Geschichte Israels*, ⁶1966; E.T., *The History of Israel*, 1958.

81. Otto, E., *Das Mazzotfest in Gilgal*, 1975.

82. ———. "Sigmund Mowinckels Bedeutung für die gegenwärtige Liturgiedebatte. Ein Beitrag zur Applikationsproblematik biblischer Überlieferung," *Jahrbuch für Liturgik und Hymnologie* 19, 1975, pp. 19-36.

83. ———. "Erwägungen zum überlieferungsgeschichtlichen Ursprung und 'Sitz im Leben' des jahwistischen Plagenzyklus," *VT* 26, 1976, pp. 3-27.

84. ———. "Silo und Jerusalem," *ThZ* 32, 1976, pp. 65-77.

85. ———. "Jakob in Bethel. Ein Beitrag zur Geschichte der Jakobüberlieferung," *ZAW* 88, 1976, pp. 165-90.

86. Patsch, H., *Abendmahl und historischer Jesus*, 1972.

87. Perrin, N., *Was lehrte Jesus Wirklich?*, 1972; E.T., *Rediscovering the Teaching of Jesus*, 1969.

88. Pesch, R., *Das Markusevangelium*, HThK II.1, 1964-65.

89. von Rad, *Theologie des Alten Testaments I/II*, 1972; E.T., *Old Testament Theology*, 2 vols. 1962-65.

90. ———. "Das Formgeschichtliche Problem des Hexateuch," *Ges. Studien*, ³1965, pp. 9-86; E.T., *The Problem of the Hexateuch and Other Essays*, 1966.

91. Reicke, B., *Diakonie, Festfreude und Zelos in Verbindung mit der altkirchlichen Agapenfeier*, 1951.

92. Rendtorff, R., *Das Gesetz in der Priesterschrift*, ³1963.

93. Rost, L., "Weidewechsel und altisraelitischer Festkalender," zdpv 66, 1943, pp. 205-15.

94. Schmithals, W., *Die Gnosis in Korinth*, ²1965; E.T., *Gnosticism in Corinth*, 1969.

95. Schniewind, J., *Die Freude der Busse*, 1956.

96. Schramm, T., *Der Markus-Stoff bei Lukas*, 1971.

97. Schweitzer, E., "Formgeschichtliches zu den Seligprei-sungen Jesu," *NTS* 19, 1972, pp. 121-26.

98. Segal, J.B., *The Hebrew Passover from the Earliest Times to A.D. 70*, 1963.

99. Sölle, D., *Leiden*, 1973; E.T., *Suffering*, 1975.

100. Soggin, J.A., "Gilgal, Pascha und Landnahme," *VT* Suppl. 15, 1966, pp. 262-77.

101. Steck, O. H., *Israel und das gewaltsame Geschick der Propheten*, 1967.

102. Stoltz, F., *Strukturen und Figuren im Kult von Jerusalem*, 1970.

103. Theissen, G., "Wanderradikalismus. Literatursoziolo-gische Aspekte der Überlieferung von Worten Jesu im Urchristentum," *ZThK* 70, 1973, pp. 245-71.

104. de Vaux, D., *Das Alte Testament und seine Lebensord-nungen* I/II, ²1964-66; E.T., *Ancient Israel; Its Life and Institutions*, 1961.

105. ———. *Les sacrifices de l'Ancien Testament*, 1964; E.T., *Studies in Old Testament Sacrifices*, 1964.

106. Via, D. O., *Die Gleichnisse Jesu*, 1970; E.T., *The Parables*, 1974.

107. Wendland, H. D., "Feste und Feiern," *RGG³*, pp. 917-19.

108. Weiser, A., "Zur Frage nach den Beziehungen der Psalmen zum Kult," *Festschrift Bertholet*, 1950, pp. 513-31.

109. ———. *Die Psalmen*, ATD 14/15, ⁷1966; E.T., *The Psalms*, 1962.

110. Westermann, C., *Das Loben Gottes in den Psalmen*, 1954; E.T., *The Praise of God in the Psalms*, 1965.

111. Wiefel, E., *Der Synagogengottesdienst im neutestament-lichen Zeitalter und seine Einwirkung auf den entstehen-*

den christlichen Gottesdienst, Diss. Theol. Leipzig, 1959.

112. Wilcoxen, J. A., "Narrative Structure and Cult-Legend. A Study of Joshua 1-6," *Transitions in Biblical Scholarship. Essays in Divinity* 6, 1968, pp. 43-70.

113. Wilkinson, J., "Ancient Jerusalem," *PEQ* 106, 1974, pp. 33-51.